ISBN 978-1-333-71577-9
PIBN 10538535

This book is a reproduction of an important historical work. Forgotten Books uses
state-of-the-art technology to digitally reconstruct the work, preserving the original format
whilst repairing imperfections present in the aged copy. In rare cases, an imperfection in
the original, such as a blemish or missing page, may be replicated in our edition. We do,
however, repair the vast majority of imperfections successfully; any imperfections that
remain are intentionally left to preserve the state of such historical works.

1 MONTH OF
FREE
READING

at
www.ForgottenBooks.com

By purchasing this book you are eligible for one month membership to ForgottenBooks.com, giving you unlimited access to our entire collection of over 700,000 titles via our web site and mobile apps.

To claim your free month visit:
www.forgottenbooks.com/free538535

English
Français
Deutsche
Italiano
Español
Português

www.forgottenbooks.com

Mythology Photography **Fiction**
Fishing Christianity **Art** Cooking
Essays Buddhism Freemasonry
Medicine **Biology** Music **Ancient**
Egypt Evolution Carpentry Physics
Dance Geology **Mathematics** Fitness
Shakespeare **Folklore** Yoga Marketing
Confidence Immortality Biographies
Poetry **Psychology** Witchcraft
Electronics Chemistry History **Law**
Accounting **Philosophy** Anthropology
Alchemy Drama Quantum Mechanics
Atheism Sexual Health **Ancient History**
Entrepreneurship Languages Sport
Paleontology Needlework Islam
Metaphysics Investment Archaeology
Parenting Statistics Criminology
Motivational

The Temple Library

SELECT ESSAYS OF
DR. JOHNSON

This *Edition is limited to Seven Hundred and Fifty*
· *copies for England, and Five Hundred copies for*
America (acquired by Messrs. Macmillan and Co.).
There is also an Edition on large paper, limited to
Two Hundred and Fifty copies.

J. M. DENT & Co.

SELECT ESSAYS

OF

R JOHNS

EDITED BY

GEORGE BIRKBECK HILL, D.C.L.

Pembroke College, Oxford

WITH ETCHINGS BY

HERBERT RAILTON

VOL. II

LONDON

M. DEN٭ ٭٭

69 GREAT RUSSELL STREET

SELECT ESSAYS

OF

JOHNS

❖❖❖

EDITED BY

GEORGE BIRKBECK HILL, D.C.L.

Pembroke College, Oxford

WITH ETCHINGS BY

HERBERT RAILTON

VOL. II

LONDON

DENT AND CO.

69 GREAT EASTERN STREET

1889

CONTENTS.

THE IDLER.

LIST OF ILLUSTRATIONS.

THE RAMBLER.

No. 148. SATURDAY, AUGUST 17, 1751.

Me pater sævis oneret catenis
Quod viro clemens misero peperci,
Me vel extremos Numidarum in agros
Classe releget.—Hor.[1]

Me let my father load with chains,
Or banish to Numidia's farthest plains!
My crime, that I, a loyal wife,
In kind compassion, sav'd my husband's life.—*Francis.*

POLITICIANS remark, that no oppression is so heavy or lasting as that which is inflicted by the perversion and exorbitance of legal authority. The robber may be seized, and the invader repelled, whenever they are found; they who pretend no right but that of force, may by force be punished or suppressed. But when plunder bears the name of impost, and murder is perpetrated by a judicial sentence, fortitude is intimidated, and wisdom confounded: resistance

[1] Horace, 3 *Odes,* xi. 45.

shrinks from an alliance with rebellion, and the villain remains secure in the robes of the magistrate.[1]

Equally dangerous and equally detestable are the cruelties often exercised in private families, under the venerable sanction of parental authority[2]; the power which we are taught to honour from the first moments of reason ; which is guarded from insult and violation by all that can impress awe upon the mind of man ; and which therefore may wanton in cruelty without controul, and trample the bounds of right with innumerable transgressions, before duty and piety will dare to seek redress, or think themselves at liberty to recur to any other means of deliverance than supplications by which insolence is elated, and tears by which cruelty is gratified.

It was for a long time imagined by the Romans, that no son could be the murderer of his father ; and they had therefore no punishment appropriated to parricide. They seem likewise to have believed with equal confidence, that no father could be cruel to his child ; and therefore they allowed every man the supreme judicature in his own house, and put the lives of his offspring into his

---

1 " Robes and furr'd gowns hide all."
—*King Lear*, Act iv., sc. 6, l. 169.

2 In The *Rambler*, No. 39, Johnson, considering the harsh control often exercised by parents over their daughters in marrying, says:—" It may be urged in extenuation of this crime which parents, not in any other respect to be numbered with robbers and assassins, frequently commit, that, in their estimation, riches and happiness are equivalent terms."

hands. But experience informed them by degrees, that they determined too hastily in favour of human nature ; they found that instinct and habit were not able to contend with avarice or malice ; that the nearest relation might be violated ; and that power, to whomsoever intrusted, might be ill employed. They were therefore obliged to supply and to change their institutions ; to deter the parricide by a new law, and to transfer capital punishments from the parent to the magistrate.

There are indeed many houses which it is impossible to enter familiarly, without discovering that parents are by no means exempt from the intoxications of dominion ; and that he who is in no danger of hearing remonstrances but from his own conscience, will seldom be long without the art of controuling his convictions, and modifying justice by his own will.

If in any situation the heart were inaccessible to malignity, it might be supposed to be sufficiently secured by parental relation. To have voluntarily become to any being the occasion of its existence, produces an obligation to make that existence happy. To see helpless infancy stretching out her hands, and pouring out her cries in testimony of dependence, without any powers to alarm jealousy, or any guilt to alienate affection must surely awaken tenderness in every human mind ; and tenderness once excited will be hourly increased by the natural contagion of felicity, by the repercussion of communicated pleasure, by the consciousness of the dignity of benefaction. I believe no generous or benevolent man can see

the vilest animal courting his regard, and shrink-
ing at his anger, playing his gambols of delight
before him, calling on him in distress, and flying
to him in danger, without more kindness than he
can persuade himself to feel for the wild and
unsocial inhabitants of the air and water. We
naturally endear to ourselves those to whom we
impart any kind of pleasure, because we imagine
their affection and esteem secured to us by the
benefits which they receive.

There is, indeed, another method by which
the pride of superiority may be likewise gratified.
He that has extinguished all the sensations of
humanity, and has no longer any satisfaction in
the reflection that he is loved as the distributor of
happiness, may please himself with exciting terror
as the inflictor of pain : he may delight his
solitude with contemplating the extent of his
power and the force of his commands; in
imagining the desires that flutter on the tongue
which is forbidden to utter them, or the discontent
which preys on the heart in which fear confines
it : he may amuse himself with new contrivances
of detection, multiplications of prohibition, and
varieties of punishment ; and swell with exultation
when he considers how little of the homage that
he receives he owes to choice.

That princes of this character have been known, the
history of all absolute kingdoms will inform us ; and
since, as Aristotle observes, ἡ οἰκονομικὴ μοναρχία,
the government of a family is naturally monarchical,[1]

---

[1] Johnson refers, I think, to the *Politics,* bk. iii., ch. 14,
15 ; but the exact words which he quotes are not found there.

it is, like other monarchies, too often arbitrarily administered. The regal and parental tyrant differ only in the extent of their dominions, and the number of their slaves. The same passions cause the same miseries; except that seldom any prince, however despotic, has so far shaken off all awe of the public eye, as to venture upon those freaks of injustice, which are sometimes indulged under the secrecy of a private dwelling. Capricious injunctions, partial decisions, unequal allotments, distributions of reward, not by merit, but by fancy, and punishments, regulated not by the degree of the offence, but by the humour of the judge, are too frequent where no power is known but that of a father.

That he delights in the misery of others, no man will confess, and yet what other motive can make a father cruel? The king may be instigated by one man to the destruction of another; he may sometimes think himself endangered by the virtues of a subject; he may dread the successful general or the popular orator; his avarice may point out golden confiscations; and his guilt may whisper that he can only be secure by cutting off all power of revenge.

But what can a parent hope from the oppression of those who were born to his protection, of those who can disturb him with no competition, who can enrich him with no spoils? Why cowards are cruel may be easily discovered; but for what reason, not more infamous than cowardice, can that man delight in oppression who has nothing to fear?

The unjustifiable severity of a parent is loaded
with this aggravation, that those whom he injures
are always in his sight.   The injustice of a prince
is often exercised upon those of whom he never
had any personal or particular knowledge ; and
the sentence which he pronounces, whether of
banishment, imprisonment, or death, removes
from his view the man whom he condemns.   But
the domestic oppressor dooms himself to gaze
upon those faces which he clouds with terror and
with sorrow ; and beholds every moment the
effects of his own barbarities.   He that can bear
to give continual pain to those who surround him,
and can walk with satisfaction in the gloom of his
own presence ; he that can see submissive misery
without relenting, and meet without emotion the
eye that implores mercy, or demands justice, will
scarcely be amended by remonstrance or admonition ; he has found means of stopping the avenues
of tenderness, and arming his heart against the
force of reason.

Even though no consideration should be paid
to the great law of social beings, by which every
individual is commanded to consult the happiness
of others, yet the harsh parent is less to be
vindicated than any other criminal, because he
less provides for the happiness of himself.   Every
man, however little he loves others, would willingly
be loved ; every man hopes to live long, and
therefore hopes for that time at which he shall
sink back to imbecility, and must depend for ease
and cheerfulness upon the officiousness of others.
But how has he obviated the inconveniencies of

old age, who alienates from him the assistance of his children, and whose bed must be surrounded in the last hours, in the hours of languor and dejection, of impatience and of pain, by strangers to whom his life is indifferent, or by enemies to whom his death is desirable?

Piety will, indeed, in good minds overcome provocation, and those who have been harassed by brutality will forget the injuries which they have suffered, so far as to perform the last duties with alacrity and zeal. But surely no resentment can be equally painful with kindness thus undeserved, nor can severer punishment be imprecated upon a man not wholly lost in meanness and stupidity, than, through the tediousness of decrepitude, to be reproached by the kindness of his own children, to receive not the tribute but the alms of attendance, and to owe every relief of his miseries, not to gratitude but to mercy.

No. 159. TUESDAY, SEPTEMBER 24, 1751.

Sunt verba et voces, quibus hunc lenire dolorem
Possis, et magnam morbi deponere partem.—HOR.[1]

The power of words, and soothing sounds, appease
The raging pain, and lessen the disease.—*FRANCIS.*

THE imbecility with which Verecundulus[2] complains that the presence of a numerous assembly freezes his faculties, is particularly incident to the studious part of mankind, whose education necessarily secludes them in their earlier years from mingled converse, till, at their dismission from schools and academies, they plunge at once into the tumult of the world, and, coming forth from the gloom of solitude, are overpowered by the blaze of public life.

It is, perhaps, kindly provided by nature, that as the feathers and strength of a bird grow together, and her wings are not completed till she is able to fly, so some proportion should be preserved in the human kind between judgment and courage ; the precipitation of inexperience is therefore restrained by shame, and we remain shackled by timidity, till we have learned to speak and act with propriety.

[1] Horace, 1 *Epistles*, i. 34.
[2] The *Rambler*, No. 157, is in the form of a letter signed Verecundulus.

I believe few can review the days of their youth, without recollecting temptations, which shame, rather than virtue, enabled them to resist ; and opinions which, however erroneous in their principles, and dangerous in their consequences, they have panted to advance at the hazard of contempt and hatred, when they found themselves irresistibly depressed by a languid anxiety, which seized them at the moment of utterance, and still gathered strength from their endeavours to resist it.

It generally happens that assurance keeps an even pace with ability, and the fear of miscarriage, which hinders our first attempts, is gradually dissipated as our skill advances towards certainty of success. That bashfulness, therefore, which prevents disgrace, that short and temporary shame, which secures us from the danger of lasting reproach, cannot be properly counted among our misfortunes.

Bashfulness, however it may incommode for a moment, scarcely ever produces evils of long continuance ; it may flush the cheek, flutter in the heart, deject the eyes, and enchain the tongue, but its mischiefs soon pass off without remembrance. It may sometimes exclude pleasure, but seldom opens any avenue to sorrow or remorse. It is observed somewhere that "few have repented of having forborne to speak."

To excite opposition, and inflame malevolence, is the unhappy privilege of courage made arrogant by consciousness of strength. No man finds in himself any inclination to attack or oppose him who confesses his superiority by blushing in his presence. Qualities exerted with apparent fearfulness, receive applause from every voice, and support from every hand. Diffidence may check resolution and obstruct performance, but compensates its embarrassments by more important advantages ; it conciliates the proud, and softens the severe, averts envy from excellence, and censure from miscarriage.

It may indeed happen that knowledge and virtue remain too long congealed by this frigorific power, as the principles of vegetation are sometimes obstructed by lingering frosts. He that enters late into a public station, though with all the abilities requisite to the discharge of his duty, will find his powers at first impeded by a timidity which he himself knows to be vicious, and must struggle long against dejection and reluctance, before he obtains the full command of his own attention, and adds the gracefulness of ease to the dignity of merit.

For this disease of the mind I know not whether any remedies of much efficacy can be found. To advise a man unaccustomed to the eyes of multitudes to mount a tribunal without perturbation, to tell him whose life was passed in the shades of contemplation, that he must not be disconcerted or perplexed in receiving and returning the compliments of a splendid assembly, is to advise an inhabitant of Brasil or Sumatra not to shiver at an English winter, or him who has always lived upon a plain to look from a precipice without emotion. It is to suppose custom instantaneously

controllable by reason, and to endeavour to communicate, by precept, that which only time and
habit can bestow.

He that hopes by philosophy and contemplation alone to fortify himself against that awe
which all, at their first appearance on the stage
of life, must feel from the spectators, will, at
the hour of need, be mocked by his resolution;
and I doubt whether the preservatives which
Plato relates Alcibiades to have received from
Socrates, when he was about to speak in public,
proved sufficient to secure him from the powerful
fascination.[1]

Yet, as the effects of time may by art and
industry be accelerated or retarded, it cannot be
improper to consider how this troublesome instinct
may be opposed when it exceeds its just proportion, and, instead of repressing petulance and
temerity, silences eloquence, and debilitates force;
since, though it cannot be hoped that anxiety
should be immediately dissipated, it may be at
least somewhat abated; and the passions will
operate with less violence, when reason rises
against them, than while she either slumbers in

---

[1] " Sir William Scott mentioned that Johnson had told him
that he had several times tried to speak in the Society of Arts
and Sciences, but 'had found he could not get on.' From
Mr. William Gerard Hamilton I have heard that Johnson,
when observing to him that it was prudent for a man who had
not been accustomed to speak in public, to begin his speech in
as simple a manner as possible, acknowledged that he rose in
that society to deliver a speech which he had prepared, 'but,'
said he, 'all my flowers of oratory forsook me.'"—Boswell's
Johnson, ii. 139.

neutrality, or, mistaking her interest, lends them her assistance.

No cause more frequently produces bashfulness than too high an opinion of our own importance. He that imagines an assembly filled with his merit, panting with expectation, and hushed with attention, easily terrifies himself with the dread of disappointing them, and strains his imagination in pursuit of something that may vindicate the veracity of fame, and show that his reputation was not gained by chance. He considers that what he shall say or do will never be forgotten ; that re-nown or infamy is suspended upon every syllable, and that nothing ought to fall from him which will not bear the test of time. Under such solic -tude, who can wonder that the mind is over-whelmed, and, by struggling with attempts above her strength, quickly sinks into languishment and despondency ?

The most useful medicines are often unpleasing to the taste. Those who are oppressed by their own reputation, will, perhaps, not be comforted by hearing that their cares are unnecessary. But the truth is, that no man is much regarded by the rest of the world. He that considers how little he dwells upon the condition of others, will learn how little the attention of others is attracted by himself. While we see multitudes passing before us, of whom, perhaps, not one appears to deserve our notice, or excite our sympathy, we should remember, that we likewise are lost in the same throng ; that the eye which happens to glance upon us is turned in a moment on him that follows us, and that the utmost which we can reasonably hope or fear is, to fill a vacant hour with prattle, and be forgotten.

No. 160. SATURDAY, SEPTEMBER 28, 1751.

———*Inter se convenit ursis.*—Juv.[1]

Beasts of each kind their fellows spare;
Bear lives in amity with bear.

"THE world," says Locke, "has people of all sorts." As in the general hurry produced by the superfluities of some, and necessities of others, no man needs to stand still for want of employment, so in the innumerable gradations of ability, and endless varieties of study and inclination, no employment can be vacant for want of a man qualified to discharge it.

Such is probably the natural state of the universe ; but it is so much deformed by interest and passion, that the benefit of this adaptation of men to things is not always perceived. The folly or indigence of those who set their services to sale, inclines them to boast of qualifications which they do not possess, and attempt business which they do not not understand ; and they who have the power of assigning to others the task of life, are seldom honest or seldom happy in their

[1] Juvenal, *Satires*, xv. 164.

nomination. Patrons are corrupted by avarice, cheated by credulity, or overpowered by resistless solicitation. They are sometimes too strongly influenced by honest prejudices of friendship, or the prevalence of virtuous compassion. For, whatever cool reason may direct, it is not easy for a man of tender and scrupulous goodness to overlook the immediate effect of his own actions, by turning his eyes upon remoter consequences, and to do that which must give present pain, for the sake of obviating evil yet unfelt, or securing advantage in time to come. What is distant is in itself obscure, and, when we have no wish to see it, easily escapes our notice, or takes such a form as desire or imagination bestows upon it.

Every man might, for the same reason, in the multitudes that swarm about him, find some kindred mind with which he could unite in confidence and friendship ; yet we see many straggling single about the world, unhappy for want of an associate, and pining with the necessity of confining their sentiments to their own bosoms.

This inconvenience arises, in like manner, from struggles of the will against the understanding. It is not often difficult to find a suitable companion, if every man would be content with such as he is qualified to please. But if vanity tempts him to forsake his rank, and post himself among those with whom no common interest or mutual pleasure can ever unite him, he must always live in a state of unsocial separation, without tenderness and without trust.

There are many natures which can never approach within a certain distance, and which, when
any irregular motive impels them towards contact,
seem to start back from each other by some invincible repulsion. There are others which immediately cohere whenever they come into the reach
of mutual attraction and with very little formality
of preparation mingle intimately as soon as
they meet. Every man, whom either business or
curiosity has thrown at large into the world, will
recollect many instances of fondness and dislike,
which have forced themselves upon him without
the intervention of his judgment ; of dispositions
to court some and avoid others, when he could
assign no reason for the preference, or none
adequate to the violence of his passions ; of
influence that acted instantaneously upon his
mind, and which no arguments or persuasions
could ever overcome.

Among those with whom time and intercourse
have made us familiar, we feel our affections
divided in different proportions without much
regard to moral or intellectual merit. Every
man knows some whom he cannot induce himself
to trust, though he has no reason to suspect
that they would betray him ; those to whom
he cannot complain, though he never observed
them to want compassion ; those in whose presence he never can be gay, though excited by
invitations to mirth and freedom ; and those
from whom he cannot be content to receive
instruction, though they never insulted his
ignorance by contempt or ostentation.

That much regard is to be had to those instincts of kindness and dislike, or that reason should blindly follow them, I am far from intending to inculcate ; it is very certain, that by indulgence we may give them strength which they have not from nature, and almost every example of ingratitude and treachery proves, that by obeying them we may commit our happiness to those who are very unworthy of so great a trust. But it may deserve to be remarked, that since few contend much with their inclinations, it is generally vain to solicit the good-will of those whom we perceive thus involuntarily alienated from us ; neither knowledge nor virtue will reconcile antipathy, and though officiousness may for a time be admitted, and diligence applauded, they will at last be dismissed with coldness, or discouraged by neglect.

Some have indeed an occult power of stealing upon the affections, of exciting universal benevolence, and disposing every heart to fondness and friendship. But this is a felicity granted only to the favourites of nature. The greater part of mankind find a different reception from different dispositions ; they sometimes obtain unexpected caresses from those whom they never flattered with uncommon regard, and sometimes exhaust all their arts of pleasing without effect. To these it is necessary to look round, and attempt every breast in which they find virtue sufficient for the foundation of friendship ; to enter into the crowd, and try whom chance will offer to their notice, till they fix on some temper congenial to their own, as the magnet rolled in the dust collects the fragments of its kindred metal from a thousand particles of other substances.

Every man must have remarked the facility with which the kindness of others is sometimes gained by those to whom he never could have imparted his own. We are by our occupations, education, and habits of life, divided almost into different species, which regard one another, for the most part, with scorn and malignity.[1] Each of these classes of the human race has desires, fears, and conversation, vexations and merriment peculiar to itself; cares which another cannot feel; pleasures which he cannot partake; and modes of expressing every sensation which he cannot understand. That frolic which shakes one man with laughter, will convulse another with indignation; the strain of jocularity which in one place obtains treats and patronage, would in another be heard with indifference, and in a third with abhorrence.

To raise esteem we must benefit others, to procure love we must please them. Aristotle observes, that old men do not readily form friendships, because they are not easily susceptible of pleasure.[2] He that can contribute to the hilarity of the vacant hour, or partake with equal gust the favourite amusement; he whose mind is employed on the same objects, and who therefore

1 Johnson nearly thirty years later said :—"*F*rom my experience I have found mankind worse in commercial dealings, more disposed to cheat, than I had any notion of ; but more disposed to do one another good than I had conceived." —Boswell's *Johnson*, iii. 236.

Perhaps Johnson refers to Aristotle's *Ethics*, viii. 6, 1.

never harasses the understanding with unaccustomed ideas, will be welcomed with ardour, and
left with regret, unless he destroys those recom-
mendations by faults with which peace and security
cannot consist.

It were happy, if, in forming friendships, virtue
could concur with pleasure ; but the greatest part
of human gratifications approach so nearly to vice,
that few who make the delight of others their rule
of conduct, can avoid disingenuous compliances ;
yet certainly he that suffers himself to be driven
or allured from virtue, mistakes his own interest,
since he gains succour by means, for which his
friend, if ever he becomes wise, must scorn him,
and for which at last he must scorn himself.

No 169. TUESDAY, OCTOBER 29, 1751.

Nec pluteum cœdit, nec demorsos sapit ungues.
                                        —PERSIUS.[1]

No blood from bitten nails those poems drew ;
But churn'd, like spittle, from the lips they flew.
                                        —DRYDEN.

NATURAL historians assert, that whatever is formed for long duration arrives
slowly to its maturity. Thus the
firmest timber is of tardy growth, and
animals generally exceed each other in longevity,
in proportion to the time between their conception
and their birth.

The same observation may be extended to the

1 *Satires,* i. 106.

offspring of the mind. Hasty compositions, however they please at first by flowery luxuriance, and
spread in the sunshine of temporary favour, can
seldom endure the change of seasons, but perish
at the first blast of criticism, or frost of neglect.
When Apelles was reproached with the paucity of
his productions, and the incessant attention with
which he retouched his pieces, he condescended to
make no other answer than that *he painted for
perpetuity.*

No vanity can more justly incur contempt and
indignation than that which boasts of negligence
and hurry. For who can bear with patience the
writer who claims such superiority to the rest of
his species, as to imagine that mankind are at
leisure for attention to his extemporary sallies, and
that posterity will reposite his casual effusions
among the treasures of ancient wisdom ?

Men have sometimes appeared of such transcendent abilities, that their slightest and most
cursory performances excel all that labour and
study can enable meaner intellects to compose ;
as there are regions of which the spontaneous
products cannot be equalled in other soils by care
and culture. But it is no less dangerous for any
man to place himself in this rank of understanding, and fancy that he is born to be illustrious without labour, than to omit the cares of husbandry and
expect from his ground the blossoms of Arabia.

The greatest part of those who congratulate
themselves upon their intellectual dignity, and
usurp the privileges of genius, are men whom
only themselves would ever have marked out as

enriched by uncommon liberalities of nature, or
entitled to veneration and immortality on easy
terms.   This ardour of confidence is usually found
among those who, having not enlarged their notions
by books or conversation, are persuaded, by the
partiality which we all feel in our own favour, that
they have reached the summit of excellence,
because they discover none higher than themselves ; and who acquiesce in the first thoughts
that occur, because their scantiness of knowledge
allows them little choice ; and the narrowness of
their views affords them no glimpse of perfection,
of that sublime idea which human industry has
from the first ages been vainly toiling to approach.
They see a little, and believe that there is nothing
beyond their sphere of vision, as the Patuecos of
Spain, who inhabited a small valley, conceived the
surrounding mountains to be the boundaries of the
world.[1]   In proportion as perfection is more dis-
tinctly conceived, the pleasure of contemplating
our own performances will be lessened ; it may
therefore be observed, that they who most deserve

---

[1] Johnson refers, I think, to a passage in Howell's *Instructions for Forreine Travell* (ed. 1869, p. 51) where the author
mentions "a strange discovery that was made not much above
halfe a hundared yeares ago, about the very middle of Spaine,
of the Pattuecos, a people that were never knowne upon the
face of the Earth before. . . . Some *F*aulkners clammering up
and down, from hill to hill, and luring all along they
lighted at last upon a large pleasant valley, where they spied
a company of naked Savage people, locked in between an
assembly of huge crags and hills indented and hemmed in
(as it were) one in another."   Howell does not mention that
the Patuecos thought their mountains the boundaries of the
world.

praise are often afraid to decide in favour of their
own performances ; they know how much is still
wanting to their completion, and wait with anxiety
and terror the determination of the public. " I
please every one else (says Tully) but never
satisfy myself."

It has often been inquired, why, notwithstanding
the advances of later ages in science, and the
assistance which the infusion of so many new ideas
has given us, we fall below the ancients in the art
of composition. Some part of their superiority
may be justly ascribed to the graces of their
language, from which the most polished of the
present European tongues are nothing more than
barbarous degenerations.[1] Some advantage they
might gain merely by priority, which put them in
possession of the most natural sentiments, and left
us nothing but servile repetition or forced conceits.
But the greater part of their praise seems to have
been the just reward of modesty and labour.
Their sense of human weakness confined them
commonly to one study, which their knowledge of
the extent of every science engaged them to prosecute with indefatigable diligence.

Among the writers of antiquity I remember
none except Statius who ventures to mention the
speedy production of his writings, either as an

---

[1] Dryden in his *Essay of Dramatick Poesie* describes
how "by the inundation of the Goths and Vandals into
Italy new languages were brought in, and barbarously
mingled with the Latin, of which the Italian, Spanish, French
and ours (made out of them and the Teutonic) are dialects."
—Dryden's *Works*, ed. 1701, i. 25.

extenuation of his faults, or a proof of his facility.
Nor did Statius, when he considered himself as
a candidate for lasting reputation, think a closer
attention unnecessary, but amidst all his pride
and indigence, the two great hasteners of modern
poems, employed twelve years upon the Thebaid,
and thinks his claim to renown proportionate to
his labour.

> *Thebais, multa cruciata lima,*
> *Tentat, audaci fide, Mantuanæ*
> *Gaudia famæ.*[1]
>
> Polish'd with endless toil, my lays
> At length aspire to Mantuan praise.

Ovid indeed apologizes in his banishment for
the imperfection of his letters, but mentions his
want of leisure to polish them as an addition to
his calamities[2]; and was so far from imagining
revisals and corrections unnecessary, that at his
departure from Rome, he threw his Metamorphoses
into the fire, lest he should be disgraced by a book
which he could not hope to finish.

It seems not often to have happened that the
same writer aspired to reputation in verse and
prose ; and of those few that attempted such diver-
sity of excellence, I know not that even one suc-
ceeded. Contrary characters they never imagined
a single mind able to support, and therefore no
man is recorded to have undertaken more than one
kind of dramatic poetry.

---

[1] Statius, *Silvæ*, iv. 7, 26.
[2] Perhaps Johnson refers to *Epis. ex Ponto*, iii. 9, 49.
  " Musa mea est index nimium quoque vera malorum,
    Atque incorruptæ pondera testis habet."
Cf. also *ib.* i. 5, iv. 13, and *Tristia* i. 1.

What they had written, they did not venture in their first fondness to thrust into the world, but, considering the impropriety of sending forth inconsiderately that which cannot be recalled, deferred the publication, if not nine years, according to the direction of Horace,[1] yet till their fancy was cooled after the raptures of invention, and the glare of novelty had ceased·to dazzle the judgment.

There were in those days no weekly or diurnal writers ; *multa dies, et multa litura*[2], much time, and many rasures, were considered as indispensable requisites ; and that no other method of attaining lasting praise has been yet discovered, may be conjectured from the blotted manuscripts of Milton now remaining,[3] and from the tardy emission of Pope's compositions,[4] delayed more than once till the incidents to which they alluded were forgotten, till his enemies were secure from his satire, and what to an honest mind must be more painful, his friends were deaf to his encomiums.

To him, whose eagerness of praise hurries his productions soon into the light, many imperfections are unavoidable, even where the mind

---

[1] *Ars Poetica*, l. 388.   [2] *Ib.*, l. 293.

[3] " That in the early part of his life Milton wrote with much care appears from his manuscript, happily preserved at Cambridge, in which many of his smaller works are found as they were first written, with the subsequent corrections. Such relics show how excellence is acquired ; what we hope ever to do with ease we must learn first to do with diligence."— Johnson's *Works*, vii. 119.

[4] " Pope's publications were never hasty. He is said to have sent nothing to the press till it had lain two years under his inspection."—*Ib.*, viii. 322.

furnishes the materials, as well as regulates their dispositions, and nothing depends upon search or information. Delay opens new veins of thought, the subject dismissed for a time appears with a new train of dependent images, the accidents of reading or conversation supply new ornaments or allusions, or mere intermission of the fatigue of thinking enables the mind to collect new force, and make new excursions. But all those benefits come too late for him, who, when he was weary with labour, snatched at the recompense, and gave his work to his friends and his enemies, as soon as impatience and pride persuaded him to conclude it.

One of the most pernicious effects of haste, is obscurity. He that teems with a quick succession of ideas, and perceives how one sentiment produces another, easily believes that he can clearly express what he so strongly comprehends ; he seldom suspects his thoughts of embarrassment, while he preserves in his own memory the series of connexion, or his diction of ambiguity, while only one sense is present to his mind. Yet if he has been employed on an abstruse, or complicated argument, he will find, when he has awhile withdrawn his mind, and returns as a new reader to his work, that he has only a conjectural glimpse of his own meaning, and that to explain it to those whom he desires to instruct, he must open his sentiments, disentangle his method, and alter his arrangement.

Authors and lovers always suffer some infatuation, from which only absence can set them free ;

and every man ought to restore himself to the full
exercise of his judgment, before he does that which
he cannot do improperly, without injuring his
honour and his quiet.

No. 173. TUESDAY, NOVEMBER 12, 1751.

Quo virtus, quo ferat error ?—HOR.[1]
Now say, where virtue stops, and vice begins?

AS any action or posture, long continued,
will distort and disfigure the limbs ; so
the mind likewise is crippled and contracted by perpetual application to the
same set of ideas. It is easy to guess the trade
of an artizan by his knees, his fingers, or his
shoulders : and there are few among men of the
more liberal professions, whose minds do not carry
the brand of their calling, or whose conversation
does not quickly discover to what class of the
community they belong.

These peculiarities have been of great use, in
the general hostility which every part of mankind
exercises against the rest, to furnish insults and
sarcasms. Every art has its dialect, uncouth and
ungrateful to all whom custom has not reconciled
to its sound, and which therefore becomes
ridiculous by a slight misapplication, or unnecessary repetition.

[1] Horace, *Ars Poetica*, l. 308.

The general reproach with which ignorance revenges the superciliousness of learning, is that of pedantry ; a censure which every man incurs, who has at any time the misfortune to talk to those who cannot understand him, and by which the modest and timorous are sometimes frightened from the display of their acquisitions, and the exertion of their powers.

The name of a pedant is so formidable to young men when they first sally from their colleges, and is so liberally scattered by those who mean to boast their elegance of education, easiness of manners, and knowledge of the world, that it seems to require particular consideration ; since, perhaps, if it were once understood, many a heart might be freed from painful apprehensions, and many a tongue delivered from restraint.

Pedantry is the unseasonable ostentation of learning. It may be discovered either in the choice of a subject, or in the manner of treating it. He is undoubtedly guilty of pedantry, who, when he has made himself master of some abstruse and uncultivated part of knowledge, obtrudes his remarks and discoveries upon those whom he believes unable to judge of his proficiency, and from whom, as he cannot fear contradiction, he cannot properly expect applause.

To this error the student is sometimes betrayed by the natural recurrence of the mind to its common employment, by the pleasure which every man receives from the recollection of pleasing images, and the desire of dwelling upon topics, on which he knows himself able to speak with justness. But because we are seldom so far prejudiced in favour of each other, as to search out for palliations, this failure of politeness is imputed always to vanity; and the harmless collegiate, who, perhaps, intended entertainment and instruction, or at worst only spoke without sufficient reflection upon the character of his hearers, is censured as arrogant or overbearing, and eager to extend his renown, in contempt of the convenience of society, and the laws of conversation.

All discourse of which others cannot partake, is not only an irksome usurpation of the time devoted to pleasure and entertainment, but what never fails to excite very keen resentment, an insolent assertion of superiority, and a triumph over less enlightened understandings. The pedant is, therefore, not only heard with weariness, but malignity; and those who conceive themselves insulted by his knowledge, never fail to tell with acrimony how injudiciously it was exerted.

To avoid this dangerous imputation, scholars sometimes divest themselves with too much haste of their academical formality, and in their endeavours to accommodate their notions and their style to common conceptions, talk rather of any thing than of that which they understand, and sink into insipidity of sentiment and meanness of expression.

There prevails among men of letters an opinion that all appearance of science is particularly hateful to women; and that therefore, whoever desires to be well received in female assemblies, must qualify himself by a total rejection of all that is serious, rational, or important ; must consider argument or criticism, as perpetually interdicted ; and devote all his attention to trifles, and all his eloquence to compliment.

Students often form their notions of the present generation from the writings of the past, and are not very early informed of those changes which the gradual diffusion of knowledge, or the sudden caprice of fashion, produces in the world. Whatever might be the state of female literature in the last century, there is now no longer any danger lest the scholar should want an adequate audience at the tea-table[1] ; and whoever thinks it necessary to regulate his conversation by antiquated rules, will be rather despised for his futility than caressed for his politeness.

To talk intentionally in a manner above the comprehension of those whom we address, is unquestionable pedantry ; but surely complaisance requires, that no man should, without proof, conclude his company incapable of following him to the highest elevation of his fancy, or the utmost extent of his knowledge. It is always safer to err in favour of others than of ourselves, and

[1] " The call for books was not in Milton's age what it is in the present. To read was not then a general amusement. . .. The women had not then aspired to literature."—Johnson's *Works*, vii. 107. "That general knowledge which now circulates in common talk was in Addison's time rarely to be found. Men not professing learning were not ashamed of ignorance ; and in the female world any acquaintance with books was distinguished only to be censured."— *Ib.*, p. 470.

therefore we seldom hazard much by endeavouring to excel.[1]

It ought at least to be the care of learning, when she quits her exaltation, to descend with dignity. Nothing is more despicable than the airiness and jocularity of a man bred to severe science, and solitary meditation. To trifle agreeably is a secret which schools cannot impart; that gay negligence and vivacious levity, which charm down resistance wherever they appear, are never attainable by him who, having spent his first years among the dust of libraries, enters late into the gay world with an unpliant attention and established habits.

It is observed in the panegyric on Fabricius the mechanist,[2] that though forced by public employments into mingled conversation, he never lost the modesty and seriousness of the convent, nor drew ridicule upon himself by an affected imitation of fashionable life. To the same praise every man devoted to learning ought to aspire.

[1] " Sir Joshua once observed to Johnson that he had talked above the capacity of some people with whom they had been in company together. ' No matter, sir (said Johnson) ; they consider it as a compliment to be talked to as if they were wiser than they are. So true is this, sir, that Baxter made it a rule in every sermon that he preached to say something that was above the capacity of his audience.' "—Boswell's *Johnson*, iv. 185.

[2] In the first edition *mechanician*. If the correction is Johnson's it is of some interest, as *mechanist* is not in his *Dictionary*. Among the numerous Germans of the name of Fabricius mentioned in the *Biographie Générale* I find no one so described. David Fabricius (1564—1617) an astronomer made his own instruments, and perhaps he is meant.

If he attempts the softer arts of pleasing, and
endeavours to learn the graceful bow and the
familiar embrace, the insinuating accent and the
genial smile, he will lose the respect due to the
character of learning, without arriving at the
envied honour of doing any thing with elegance
and facility.

Theophrastus was discovered not to be a native
of Athens, by so strict an adherence to the Attic
dialect, as shewed that he had learned it not by
custom, but by rule.   A man not early formed to
habitual elegance, betrays in like manner the
effects of his education, by an unnecessary anxiety
of behaviour. It is as possible to become pedantic
by fear of pedantry, as to be troublesome by ill-
timed civility.   There is no kind of impertinence
more justly censurable, than his who is always
labouring to level thoughts to intellects higher
than his own ; who apologizes for every word
which his own narrowness of converse inclines
him to think unusual ; keeps the exuberance of
his faculties under visible restraint ; is solicitous
to anticipate inquiries by needless explanations ;
and endeavours to shade his own abilities, lest
weak eyes should be dazzled with their lustre.[1]

[1] " There is (said Johnson) nothing more likely to betray
a man into absurdity than *condescension ;* when he seems to
suppose his understanding too powerful for his company."—
Boswell's *Johnson,* iv. 3.

No. 176. SATURDAY, NOVEMBER 23, 1751.

——— *Naso suspendis adunco.*—Hor.[1]

On me you turn the nose.

THERE are many vexatious accidents and uneasy situations which raise little compassion for the sufferer, and which no man but those whom they immediately distress can regard with seriousness. Petty mischiefs, that have no influence on futurity, nor extend their effects to the rest of life, are always seen with a kind of malicious pleasure. A mistake or embarrassment, which for the present moment fills the face with blushes, and the mind with confusion, will have no other effect upon those who observe it, than that of convulsing them with irresistible laughter. Some circumstances of misery are so powerfully ridiculous, that neither kindness nor duty can withstand them ; they bear down love, interest, and reverence, and force the friend, the dependant, or the child, to give away to instantaneous motions of merriment.

Among the principal of comic calamities, may be reckoned the pain which an author, not yet hardened into insensibility, feels at the onset of a furious critic, whose age, rank, or fortune, gives

[1] Horace, 1 *Satires,* vi. 5.

him confidence to speak without reserve ; who heaps one objection upon another, and obtrudes his remarks, and enforces his corrections, without tenderness or awe.

The author, full of the importance of his work, and anxious for the justification of every syllable, starts and kindles at the slightest attack ; the critic, eager to establish his superiority, triumphing in every discovery of failure, and zealous to impress the cogency of his arguments, pursues him from line to line without cessation or remorse. The critic, who hazards little, proceeds with vehemence, impetuosity, and fearlessness ; the author, whose quiet and fame, and life and immortality, are involved in the controversy, tries every art of subterfuge and defence ; maintains modestly what he resolves never to yield, and yields unwillingly what cannot be maintained. The critic's purpose is to conquer, the author only hopes to escape ; the critic therefore knits his brow, and raises his voice, and rejoices whenever he perceives any tokens of pain excited by the pressure of his assertions, or the point of his sarcasms. The author, whose endeavour is at once to mollify and elude his persecutor, composes his features and softens his accent, breaks the force of assault by retreat, and rather steps aside than flies or advances.

As it very seldom happens that the range of extemporary criticism inflicts fatal or lasting wounds, I know not that the laws of benevolence entitle this distress to much sympathy. The diversion of baiting an author has the sanction

of all ages and nations, and is more lawful than
the sport of teasing other animals, because, for
the most part, he comes voluntarily to the stake,
furnished, as he imagines, by the patron powers
of literature, with resistless weapons, and impenetrable armour, with the mail of the boar of
Erymanth, and the paws of the lion of Nemea.

But the works of genius are sometimes produced by other motives than vanity; and he
whom necessity or duty enforces to write, is not
always so well satisfied with himself, as not to
be discouraged by censorious impudence. It
may therefore be necessary to consider, how
they whom publication lays open to the insults
of such as their obscurity secures against
reprisals, may extricate themselves from unexpected en counters.

Vida,[1] a man of considerable skill in the politics
of literature, directs his pupil wholly to abandon
his defence, and even when he can irrefragably
refute all objections to suffer tamely the exulta-
tions of his antagonist.

This rule may perhaps be just, when advice
is asked, and severity solicited, because no man
tells his opinion so freely as when he imagines
it received with implicit veneration; and critics

[1] " With sweeter notes each rising temple rung;
  A Raphael painted, and a Vida sung.
  Immortal Vida ! on whose honour'd brow
  The poet's bays and critic's ivy grow."
                    —Pope, *Essay on Criticism*, l. 703.
" Christopher Pitt, probably about this time (1724), trans-
lated Vida's *Art of Poetry*, which Tristram's splendid edition
had then made popular."—Johnson's *Works*, viii. 363.

II   D

ought never to be consulted, but while errors may yet be rectified or insipidity suppressed. But when the book has once been dismissed into the world, and can be no more retouched, I know not whether a very different conduct should not be prescribed, and whether firmness and spirit may not sometimes be of use to overpower arrogance and repel brutality. Softness, diffidence, and moderation, will often be mistaken for imbecility and dejection ; they lure cowardice to the attack by the hopes of easy victory, and it will soon be found that he whom every man thinks he can conquer, shall never be at peace.[1]

The animadversions of critics are commonly such as may easily provoke the sedatest writer to some quickness of resentment and asperity of reply. A man who by long consideration has familiarized a subject to his own mind, carefully surveyed the series of his thoughts, and planned all the parts of composition into a regular dependence on each other, will often start at the sinistrous interpretations, or absurd remarks

---

1 "BOSWELL. 'Goldsmith is the better for attacks.' JOHN-SON. 'Yes, sir ; but he does not think so yet. When Goldsmith and I published each of us something at the same time, we were given to understand that we might review each other. Goldsmith was for accepting the offer. I said, No ; set reviewers at defiance. It was said to old Bentley upon the attacks against him, "Why, they'll write you down." "No, sir," he replied, "depend upon it, no man was ever written down but by himself." He observed to me afterwards that the advantages derived from attacks were chiefly in subjects of taste, where you cannot confute, as so much may be said on either side.' "—Boswell's *Johnson*, v. 274.

of haste and ignorance, and wonder by what infatuation they have been led away from the obvious sense, and upon what peculiar principles of judgment they decide against him.

The eye of the intellect, like that of the body, is not equally perfect in all, nor equally adapted in any to all objects ; the end of criticism is to supply its defects ; rules are the instruments of mental vision, which may indeed assist our faculties when properly used, but produce confusion and obscurity by unskilful application.

Some seem always to read with the microscope of criticism, and employ their whole attention upon minute elegance, or faults scarcely visible to common observation. The dissonance of a syllable, the recurrence of the same sound, the repetition of a particle, the smallest deviation from propriety, the slightest defect in construction or arrangement, swell before their eyes into enormities. As they discern with great exactness, they comprehend but a narrow compass, and know nothing of the justness of the design, the general spirit of the performance, the artifice of connexion, or the harmony of the parts ; they never conceive how small a proportion that which they are busy in contemplating bears to the whole, or how the petty inaccuracies with which they are offended, are absorbed and lost in general excellence.

Others are furnished by criticism with a telescope. They see with great clearness whatever is too remote to be discovered by the rest of mankind, but are totally blind to all that lies immediately before them. They discover in every passage some secret meaning, some remote allusion, some artful allegory, or some occult imitation, which no other reader ever suspected; but they have no perception of the cogency of arguments, the force of pathetic sentiments, the various colours of diction, or the flowery embellishments of fancy; of all that engages the attention of others, they are totally insensible, while they pry into worlds of conjecture, and amuse themselves with phantoms in the clouds.

In criticism, as in every other art, we fail sometimes by our weakness, but more frequently by our fault. We are sometimes bewildered by ignorance, and sometimes by prejudice, but we seldom deviate far from the right, but when we deliver ourselves up to the direction of vanity.

No. 178. SATURDAY, NOVEMBER 30, 1751.

Pars sanitatis velle sanari fuit.—SENECA.[1]
To yield to remedies is half the cure.

PYTHAGORAS is reported to have required from those whom he instructed in philosophy a probationary silence of five years. Whether this prohibition of speech extended to all the parts of

---

[1] *Hippolytus*, l. 250. In three editions of Johnson's *Works* which I have examined—those of 1806, 1820, and the Oxford edition of 1825—*sanari* is printed *sanaria*.

this time, as seems generally to be supposed, or was to be observed only in the school or in the presence of their master, as is more probable, it was sufficient to discover the pupil's disposition ; to try whether he was willing to pay the price of learning, or whether he was one of those whose ardour was rather violent than lasting, and who expected to grow wise on other terms than those of patience and obedience.

Many of the blessings universally desired, are very frequently wanted, because most men, when they should labour, content themselves to complain, and rather linger in a state in which they cannot be at rest, than improve their condition by vigour and resolution.

Providence has fixed the limits of human enjoyment by immovable boundaries, and has set different gratifications at such a distance from each other, that no art or power can bring them together. This great law it is the business of every rational being to understand, that life may not pass away in an attempt to make contradictions consistent, to combine opposite qualities, and to unite things which the nature of their being must always keep asunder.

Of two objects tempting at a distance on contrary sides, it is impossible to approach one but by receding from the other ; by long deliberation and dilatory projects, they may be both lost, but can never be both gained. It is, therefore, necessary to compare them, and, when we have determined the preference, to withdraw our eyes and our thoughts at once from that which reason

directs us to reject. This is more necessary, if
that which we are forsaking has the power of
delighting the senses, or firing the fancy. He
that once turns aside to the allurements of un-
lawful pleasure, can have no security that he
shall ever regain the paths of virtue.

The philosophic goddess of Boethius, having
related the story of Orpheus, who, when he had
recovered his wife from the dominions of death,
lost her again by looking back upon her in the'
confines of light, concludes with a very elegant
and forcible application. " Whoever you are that
endeavour to elevate your minds to the illumina-
tions of Heaven, consider yourselves as represented in this fable ; for he that is once so far
overcome as to turn back his eyes towards the
infernal caverns, loses at the first sight all that
influence which attracted him on high : "

> Vos hæc fabula respicit,
> Quicunque in superum diem
> Mentem ducere quæritis.
> Nam qui Tartareum in specus
> Victus lumina flexerit,
> Quidquid præcipuum trahit.
> Perdit, dum videt inferos.

It may be observed, in general, that the future
is purchased by the present. It is not possible
to secure instant or permanent happiness but by
the forbearance of some immediate gratification.
This is so evidently true with regard to the whole
of our existence, that all the precepts of theology
have no other tendency than to enforce a life of
faith ; a life regulated not by our senses but

our belief; a life in which pleasures are to be
refused for fear of invisible punishments, and
calamities sometimes to be sought, and always
endured, in hope of rewards that shall be
obtained in another state.

Even if we take into our view only that particle
of our duration which is terminated by the grave,
it will be found that we cannot enjoy one part of
life beyond the common limitations of pleasure,
but by anticipating some of the satisfaction which
should exhilarate the following years. The heat
of youth may spread happiness into wild luxuriance, but the radical vigour requisite to make it
perennial is exhausted, and all that can be hoped
afterwards is languor and sterility.

The reigning error of mankind is, that we are
not content with the conditions on which the goods
of life are granted.[1] No man is insensible of the
whole of knowledge, the advantages of health,
or the convenience of plenty, but every day shows
us those on whom the conviction is without
effect.

Knowledge is praised and desired by multitudes
whom her charms could never rouse from the
couch of sloth ; whom the faintest invitation of
pleasure draws away from their studies ; to whom

1 " Every man is to take existence on the terms on which
it is given to him. To some men it is given on condition of
not taking liberties, which other men may take without
much harm. One may drink wine, and be nothing the
worse for it : on another, wine may have effects so inflamma-
tory as to injure him both in body and mind, and perhaps
make him commit something for which he may deserve to be
hanged."—Boswell's *Johnson*, iii. 58.

any other method of wearing out the day is more eligible than the use of books, and who are more easily engaged by any conversation, than such as may rectify their notions or enlarge their comprehension.

Every man that has felt pain, knows how little all other comforts can gladden him to whom health is denied. Yet who is there does not sometimes hazard it for the enjoyment of an hour? All assemblies of jollity, all places of public entertainment, exhibit examples of strength wasting in riot, and beauty withering in irregularity; nor is it easy to enter a house in which part of the family is not groaning in repentance of past intemperance, and part admitting disease by negligence, or soliciting it by luxury.

There is no pleasure which men of every age and sect have more generally agreed to mention with contempt, than the gratifications of the palate; an entertainment so far removed from intellectual happiness, that scarcely the most shameless of the sensual herd have dared to defend it: yet even to this, the lowest of our delights, to this, though neither quick or lasting, is health with all its activity and sprightliness daily sacrificed; and for this are half the miseries endured which urge impatience to call on death.[1]

[1] "At supper this night Dr. Johnson talked of good eating with uncommon satisfaction. 'Some people,' said he, 'have a foolish way of not minding, or pretending not to mind, what they eat. For my part, I mind my belly very studiously, and very carefully; for I look upon it, that he who does not mind his belly will hardly mind anything else.' He now appeared to me *Jean Bull philosophe*, and he was for the

The whole world is put in motion by the wish for riches and the dread of poverty. Who, then, would not imagine that such conduct as will inevitably destroy what all are thus labouring to acquire, must be generally avoided? That he who spends more than he receives, must in time become indigent, cannot be doubted; but, how evident soever this consequence may appear, the spendthrift moves in the whirl of pleasure with too much rapidity to keep it before his eyes, and, in the intoxication of gaiety, grows every day poorer, without any such sense of approaching ruin as is sufficient to wake him into caution.

Many complaints are made of the misery of life; and indeed it must be confessed that we are subject to calamities by which the good and bad, the diligent and slothful, the vigilant and heedless, are equally afflicted. But surely, though some indulgence may be allowed to groans extorted by inevitable misery, no man has a right to repine at evils which, against warning, against experience, he deliberately and leisurely brings upon his own head; or to consider himself as debarred from happiness by such obstacles as resolution may break or dexterity may put aside.

---

moment, not only serious, but vehement. Yet I have heard him, upon other occasions, talk with great contempt of people who were anxious to gratify their palates; and the 206th number of his *Rambler* is a masterly essay against gulosity. His practice, indeed, I must acknowledge, may be considered as casting the balance of his different opinions upon this subject; for I never knew any man who relished good eating more than he did."—Boswell's *Johnson*, i. 467.

Great numbers who quarrel with their condition, have wanted not the power but the will to obtain a better state. They have never contemplated the difference between good and evil sufficiently to quicken aversion, or invigorate desire ; they have indulged a drowsy thoughtlessness or giddy levity; have committed the balance of choice to the management of caprice ; and when they have long accustomed themselves to receive all that chance offered them without examination, lament at last that they find themselves deceived.

No. 180. SATURDAY, DECEMBER 7, 1751.

Ταῦτ' εἰδὼς σοφὸς ἴσθι, μάτην δ' Ἐπίκουρον ἔασον
Ποῦ τὸ κενὸν ζητεῖν, καὶ τίνες αἱ μονάδες.

—AUTOMEDON.[1]

On life, on morals, be thy thoughts employed :
Leave to the schools their atoms and their void.

IT is somewhere related by Le Clerc,[2] that a wealthy trader of good understanding, having the common ambition to breed his son a scholar, carried him to an university, resolving to use his own judgment in the choice of a tutor. He had been

1 Jacobs' *Anthologia Græca*, ed. 1814, ii. 335. Automedon, a Greek poet, lived in the reign of Nerva, A.D. 96-98.—Smith's *Classical Dictionary*.

2 "The celebrated John Le Clerc was now [1710] in the full career of literary ambition : in his countless publications he not only appeared as a theologian, philosopher, scholar,

taught, by whatever intelligence, the nearest way
to the heart of an academic, and at his arrival
entertained all who came about him with such
profusion, that the professors were lured by the
smell of his table from their books, and flocked
round him with all the cringes of awkward complaisance. This eagerness answered the merchant's
purpose : he glutted them with delicacies, and
softened them with caresses, till he prevailed upon
one after another to open his bosom, and make
a discovery of his competitions, jealousies, and
resentments. Having thus learned each man's
character, partly from himself, and partly from
his acquaintances, he resolved to find some other
education for his son, and went away convinced,
that a scholastic life has no other tendency than
to vitiate the morals and contract the understanding : nor would he afterwards hear with patience
the praises of the ancient authors, being persuaded
that scholars of all ages must have been the same,
and that Xenophon and Cicero were professors of
some former university, and therefore mean and
selfish, ignorant and servile, like those whom he
had lately visited and forsaken.

Envy, curiosity, and a sense of the imperfection
of our present state, incline us to estimate the

and critic, but pretended to the foremost rank in all those
different departments. He seems to have been the first
person who understood the power which may be exercised
over literature by a reviewer."—Monk's *Life of Bentley*, i.
267. Johnson, who at one time had a scheme for a Literary
Journal, wrote down in his memorandum book, "Imitate Le
Clerk."—Boswell's *Johnson*, i. 284.

advantages which are in the possession of others above their real value. Every one must have remarked, what powers and prerogatives the vulgar imagine to be conferred by learning. A man of science is expected to excel the unlettered and unenlightened even on occasions where literature is of no use, and among weak minds, loses part of his reverence, by discovering no superiority in those parts of life, in which all are unavoidably equal; as when a monarch makes a progress to the remoter provinces, the rustics are said sometimes to wonder that they find him of the same size with themselves.

These demands of prejudice and folly can never be satisfied; and therefore many of the imputations which learning suffers from disappointed ignorance, are without reproach. But there are some failures, to which men of study are peculiarly exposed. Every condition has its disadvantages. The circle of knowledge is too wide for the most active and diligent intellect, and while science is pursued, other accomplishments are neglected; as a small garrison must leave one part of an extensive fortress naked, when an alarm calls them to another.

The learned, however, might generally support their dignity with more success, if they suffered not themselves to be misled by the desire of superfluous attainment. Raphael, in return to Adam's inquiries into the courses of the stars, and the revolutions of heaven, counsels him to withdraw his mind from idle speculations, and employ his faculties upon nearer and more

interesting objects, the survey of his own life,
the subjection of his passions, the knowledge
of duties which must daily be performed, and
the detection of dangers which must daily be
incurred.[1]

This angelic counsel every man of letters should
always have before him. He that devotes himself to retired study naturally sinks from omission
to forgetfulness of social duties ; he must be therefore sometimes awakened and recalled to the
general condition of mankind.

I am far from any intention to limit curiosity,
or confine the labours of learning to arts of immediate and necessary use. It is only from the
various essays of experimental industry, and the
vague excursions of minds sent out upon discovery
that any advancement of knowledge can be expected ; and, though many must be disappointed
in their labours, yet they are not to be charged
with having spent their time in vain ; their
example contributed to inspire emulation, and
their miscarriages taught others the way to
success.

But the distant hope of being one day useful
or eminent, ought not to mislead us too far from
that study which is equally requisite to the great
and mean, to the celebrated and obscure ; the

[1] " To ask or search I blame thee not ; for heav'n
Is as the book of God before thee set,
Wherein to read his wondrous works, and learn
His seasons, hours, or days, or months, or years.
This to attain, whether heav'n move, or earth,
Imports not, if thou reckon right," &c.
—*Paradise Lost*, viii. 66.

art of moderating the desires, of repressing the appetites, and of conciliating or retaining the favour of mankind.

No man can imagine the course of his own life, or the conduct of the world around him, unworthy his attention ; yet, among the sons of learning, many seem to have thought of every thing rather than of themselves, and to have observed every thing but what passes before their eyes : Many who toil through the intricacy of complicated systems, are insuperably embarrassed with the least perplexity in common affairs ; many who compare the actions, and ascertain the characters of ancient heroes, let their own days glide away without examination, and suffer vicious habits to encroach upon their minds without resistance or detection.

The most frequent reproach of the scholastic race is the want of fortitude, not martial but philosophic. Men bred in shades and silence, taught to immure themselves at sunset, and accustomed to no other weapon than syllogism, may be allowed to feel terror at personal danger, and to be disconcerted by tumult and alarm. But why should he whose life is spent in contemplation, and whose business is only to discover truth, be unable to rectify the fallacies of imagination, or contend successfully against prejudice and passion ? To what end has he read and meditated, if he gives up his understanding to false appearances, and suffers himself to be enslaved by fear of evils to which only folly or vanity can expose him, or elated by advantages to which, as they are equally conferred upon the good and bad, no real dignity is annexed.

Such, however, is the state of the world, that the most obsequious of the slaves of pride, the most rapturous of the gazers upon wealth, the most officious of the whisperers of greatness, are collected from seminaries appropriated to the study of wisdom and of virtue, where it was intended that appetite should learn to be content with little, and that hope should aspire only to honours which no human power can give or take away.

The student, when he comes forth into the world, instead of congratulating himself upon his exemption from the errors of those whose opinions have been formed by accident or custom, and who live without any certain principles of conduct, is commonly in haste to mingle with the multitude, and show his sprightliness and ductility by an expeditious compliance with fashions or vices. The first smile of a man, whose fortune gives him power to reward his dependants, commonly enchants him beyond resistance ; the glare of equipage, the sweets of luxury, the liberality of general promises, the softness of habitual affability, fill his imagination ; and he soon ceases to have any other wish than to be well received, or any measure of right and wrong but the opinion of his patron.

A man flattered and obeyed, learns to exact grosser adulation, and enjoin lower submission. Neither our virtues nor vices are all our own. If there were no cowardice, there would be little insolence ; pride cannot rise to any great degree but by the concurrence of blandishment or the sufferance of tameness. The wretch who would shrink and crouch before one that should dart his eyes upon him with the spirit of natural equality, becomes capricious and tyrannical when he sees himself approached with a downcast look, and hears the soft address of awe and servility. To those who are willing to purchase favour by cringes and compliance, is to be imputed the haughtiness that leaves nothing to be hoped by firmness and integrity.

If, instead of wandering after the meteors of philosophy, which fill the world with splendour for a while, and then sink and are forgotten, the candidates of learning fixed their eyes upon the permanent lustre of moral and religious truth, they would find a more certain direction to happiness. A little plausibility of discourse, and acquaintance with unnecessary speculations, is dearly purchased, when it excludes those instructions which fortify the heart with resolution, and exalt the spirit to independence.

No. 185. TUESDAY, DECEMBER 24, 1751.

At vindicta bonum vita jucundius ipsa.
Nempe hoc indocti.———— ————
Chrysippus non dicit idem, nec mite Thaletis
Ingenium, dulcique senex vicinus Hymetto,
Qui partem acceptæ sæva inter vincla Cicutæ
Accusatori nollet dare.————*Quippe minuti*
Semper et infirmi est animi exiguique voluptas
Ultio.—Juv.[1]

But O ! revenge is sweet,
Thus think the crowd ; who, eager to engage,
Take quickly fire, and kindle into rage.
Not so mild *Thales* nor *Chrysippus* thought,
Nor that good man, who drank the pois'nous draught
With mind serene ; and could not wish to see
His vile accuser drink as deep as he :
Exalted Socrates ! divinely brave !
Injur'd he fell, and dying he forgave,
Too noble for revenge ; which still we find
The weakest frailty of a feeble mind.—DRYDEN.[2]

NO vicious dispositions of the mind more obstinately resist both the counsels of philosophy and the injunctions of religion, than those which are complicated with an opinion of dignity ; and which we cannot dismiss without leaving in the hands of opposition some advantage iniquitously obtained,

[1] Juvenal, *Satires*, xiii. 180.
[2] It was not Dryden, but Creech, who translated this Satire.—See Johnson's *Works*, vii. 332.

or suffering from our own prejudices some
imputation of pusillanimity.

For this reason scarcely any law of our
Redeemer is more openly transgressed, or more
industriously evaded, than that by which he
commands his followers to forgive injuries, and
prohibits, under the sanction of eternal misery,
the gratification of the desire which every man
feels to return pain upon him that inflicts it.
Many who could have conquered their anger, are
unable to combat pride, and pursue offences to
extremity of vengeance, lest they should be insulted by the triumph of an enemy.

But certainly no precept could better become
him, at whose birth peace was proclaimed to the
earth. For, what would so soon destroy all the
order of society, and deform life with violence and
ravage, as a permission to every one to judge his
own cause, and to apportion his own recompense
for imagined injuries?

It is difficult for a man of the strictest justice
not to favour himself too much, in the calmest
moments of solitary meditation. Every one
wishes for the distinctions for which thousands
are wishing at the same time, in their own opinion,
with better claims. He that, when his reason
operates in its full force, can thus, by the mere
prevalence of self-love, prefer himself to his fellow-
beings, is very unlikely to judge equitably when
his passions are agitated by a sense of wrong, and
his attention wholly engrossed by pain, interest,
or danger. Whoever arrogates to himself the
right of vengeance, shows how little he is qualified

to decide his own claims, since he certainly demands what he would think unfit to be granted to another.

Nothing is more apparent than that, however injured, or however provoked, some must at last be contented to forgive. For it can never be hoped that he who first commits an injury, will contentedly acquiesce in the penalty required : the same haughtiness of contempt, or vehemence of desire, that prompt the act of injustice, will more strongly incite its justification ; and resentment can never so exactly balance the punishment with the fault, but there will remain an overplus of vengeance which even he who condemns his first action will think himself entitled to retaliate. What then can ensue but a continual exacerbation of hatred, an unextinguishable feud, an incessant reciprocation of mischief, a mutual vigilance to entrap, and eagerness to destroy ?

Since then the imaginary right of vengeance must be at last remitted, because it is impossible to live in perpetual hostility, and equally impossible that of two enemies, either should first think himself obliged by justice to submission, it is surely eligible to forgive early. Every passion is more easily subdued before it has been long accustomed to possession of the heart ; every idea is obliterated with less difficulty, as it has been more slightly impressed, and less frequently renewed. He who has often brooded over his wrongs, pleased himself with schemes of malignity, and glutted his pride with the fancied supplications of humbled enmity, will not easily open his bosom to amity and reconciliation, or indulge the gentle sentiments of benevolence and peace.

It is easiest to forgive, while there is yet little to be forgiven. A single injury may be soon dismissed from the memory ; but a long succession of ill offices by degrees associates itself with every idea ; a long contest involves so many circumstances, that every place and action will recall it to the mind, and fresh remembrance of vexation must still enkindle rage, and irritate revenge.

A wise man will make haste to forgive, because he knows the true value of time, and will not suffer it to pass away in unnecessary pain. He that willingly suffers the corrosions of inveterate hatred, and gives up his days and nights to the gloom of malice, and perturbations of stratagem, cannot surely be said to consult his ease. Resentment is an union of sorrow with malignity,[1] a combination of a passion which all endeavour to avoid, with a passion which all concur to detest. The man who retires to meditate mischief, and to exasperate his own rage ; whose thoughts are employed only on means of distress and contrivances of ruin ; whose mind never pauses from the remembrance of his own sufferings, but to indulge some hope of enjoying the calamities of another, may justly be numbered among the most

[1] Johnson in his *Dictionary* more properly defines *resentment* as *a deep sense of injury*. It is in this sense that he uses the word in a letter to Boswell :—"Langton is a worthy fellow, without malice, though not without resentment."— Boswell's *Johnson*, ii. 292.

miserable of human beings, among those who are guilty without reward, who have neither the gladness of prosperity, nor the calm of innocence.

Whoever consider the weakness both of himself and others, will not long want persuasives[1] to forgiveness. We know not to what degree of malignity any injury is to be imputed ; or how much its guilt, if we were to inspect the mind of him that committed it, would be extenuated by mistake, precipitance, or negligence ; we cannot be certain how much more we feel than was intended to be inflicted, or how much we increase the mischief to ourselves by voluntary aggravations. We may charge to design the effects of accident ; we may think the blow violent only because we have made ourselves delicate and tender ; we are on every side in danger of error and of guilt ; which we are certain to avoid only by speedy forgiveness.

From this pacific and harmless temper, thus propitious to others and ourselves, to domestic tranquillity and to social happiness, no man is withheld but by pride, by the fear of being insulted by his adversary, or despised by the world.

It may be laid down as an unfailing and universal axiom, that "all pride is abject and "mean." It is always an ignorant, lazy, or cowardly

---

[1] This word, used as a substantive, is not in Johnson's *Dictionary*. "He assured me," writes Boswell, "that he had not taken upon him to add more than four or five words to the English language, of his own formation."—Boswell's *Johnson*, i. 221.

acquiescence in a false appearance of excellence, and proceeds not from consciousness of our attainments, but insensibility of our wants.

Nothing can be great which is not right. Nothing which reason condemns can be suitable to the dignity of the human mind. To be driven by external motives from the path which our own heart approves, to give way to any thing but conviction, to suffer the opinion of others to rule our choice, or overpower our resolves, is to submit tamely to the lowest and most ignominious slavery, and to resign the right of directing our own lives.

The utmost excellence at which humility can arrive, is a constant and determinate pursuit of virtue, without regard to present dangers or advantage ; a continual reference of every action to the divine will ; an habitual appeal to everlasting justice ; and an unvaried elevation of the intellectual eye to the reward which perseverance only can obtain. But that pride which many, who presume to boast of generous sentiments, allow to regulate their measures, has nothing nobler in view than the approbation of men, of beings whose superiority we are under no obligation to acknowledge, and who, when we have courted them with the utmost assiduity, can confer no valuable or permanent reward ; of beings who ignorantly judge of what they do not understand, or partially determine what they never have examined ; and whose sentence is therefore of no weight till it has received the ratification of our own conscience.

He that can descend to bribe suffrages like

these, at the price of his innocence ; he that can suffer the delight of such acclamations to withhold his attention from the commands of the universal Sovereign, has little reason to congratulate himself upon the greatness of his mind ; whenever he awakes to seriousness and reflection, he must become despicable in his own eyes, and shrink with shame from the remembrance of his cowardice and folly.

Of him that hopes to be forgiven, it is indispensably required that he forgive. It is therefore superfluous to urge any other motive. On this great duty eternity is suspended, and to him that refuses to practice it, the throne of mercy is inaccessible, and the SAVIOUR of the world has been born in vain.

No. 196. SATURDAY, FEBRUARY 1, 1752.

Multa ferunt anni venientes commoda secum,
*Multa recedentes adimunt.—*Hor.[1]

The blessings flowing in with life's full tide,
Down with our ebb of life decreasing glide.—*Francis.*

BAXTER, in the narrative of his own life, has enumerated several opinions, which, though he thought them evident and incontestable at his first entrance into the world, time and experience disposed him to change.[2]

Whoever reviews the state of his own mind from the dawn of manhood to its decline, and considers what he pursued or dreaded, slighted or esteemed, at different periods of his age, will have no reason to imagine such changes of sentiment peculiar to any station or character. Every man, however careless and inattentive, has conviction forced upon him; the lectures of time obtrude themselves upon the most unwilling or dissipated auditor; and, by comparing our past with our

[1] Horace, *Ars Poetica*, l. 175.

[2] "When I peruse the writings which I wrote in my younger years I can find the footsteps of my unfurnished mind, and of my emptiness and insufficiency; so that the man that followed my judgment then was likelier to have been misled by me than he that should follow it now."—*Life of Richard Baxter*, by Rev. J. H. Davies, p. 435. In the pages that follow Baxter enumerates the opinions which he had changed.

present thoughts, we perceive that we have changed our minds, though perhaps we cannot discover when the alteration happened, or by what causes it was produced.

This revolution of sentiments occasions a perpetual contest between the old and young. They who imagine themselves entitled to veneration by the prerogative of longer life, are inclined to treat the notions of those whose conduct they superintend with superciliousness and contempt, for want of considering that the future and the past have different appearances; that the disproportion will always be great between expectation and enjoyment, between new possession and satiety; that the truth of many maxims of age gives too little pleasure to be allowed till it is felt; and that the miseries of life would be increased beyond all human power of endurance, if we were to enter the world with the same opinions as we carry from it.

We naturally indulge those ideas that please us. Hope will predominate in every mind, till it has been suppressed by frequent disappointments. The youth has not yet discovered how many evils are continually hovering about us, and when he is set free from the shackles of discipline, looks abroad into the world with rapture; he sees an elysian region open before him, so variegated with beauty, and so stored with pleasure, that his care is rather to accumulate good, than to shun evil; he stands distracted by different forms of delight, and has no other doubt, than which path to follow of those which all lead equally to the bowers of happiness.

He who has seen only the superficies of life believes every thing to be what it appears, and rarely suspects that external splendour conceals any latent sorrow or vexation. He never imagines that there may be greatness without safety, affluence without content, jollity without friendship, and solitude without peace. He fancies himelf permitted to cull the blessings of every condition, and to leave its inconveniences to the idle and the ignorant. He is inclined to believe no man miserable but by his own fault, and seldom looks with much pity upon failings or miscarriages, because he thinks them willingly admitted, or negligently incurred.

It is impossible, without pity and contempt, to hear a youth of generous sentiments and warm imagination, declaring, in the moment of openness and confidence, his designs and expectations; because long life is possible, he considers it as certain, and therefore promises himself all the changes of happiness, and provides gratifications for every desire. He is, for a time, to give himself wholly to frolic and diversion, to range the world in search of pleasure, to delight every eye, to gain every heart, and to be celebrated equally for his pleasing levities and solid attainments, his deep reflections and his sparkling repartees. He then elevates his views to nobler enjoyments, and finds all the scattered excellencies of the female world united in a woman, who prefers his addresses to wealth and titles ; he is afterwards to engage in business, to dissipate difficulty, and overpower opposition : to climb, by the mere force of merit,

to fame and greatness ; and reward all those who
countenance his rise, or paid due regard to his
early excellence. At last he will retire in peace
and honour ; contract his views to domestic pleasures ; form the manners of children like himself ;
observe how every year expands the beauty of
his daughters, and how his sons catch ardour
from their father's history ; he will give laws to
the neighbourhood ; dictate axioms to posterity ;
and leave the world an example of wisdom and of
happiness.

With hopes like these, he sallies jocund into
life ; to little purpose is he told, that the condition
of humanity admits no pure and unmingled happiness ; that the exuberant gaiety of youth ends
in poverty or disease ; that uncommon qualifications and contrarities of excellence, produce envy
equally with applause ; that, whatever admiration
and fondness may promise him, he must marry
a wife like the wives of others, with some virtues
and some faults, and be as often disgusted by her
vices, as delighted by her elegance ; that if
he adventures into the circle of action, he must
expect to encounter men as artful, as daring, as
resolute as himself ; that of his children, some
may be deformed, and others vicious ; some may
disgrace him by their follies, some offend him
by their insolence, and some exhaust him by their
profusion. He hears all this with obstinate incre-
dulity, and wonders bv what malignity old age is
influenced, that it cannot forbear to fill his ears
with predictions of misery.

Among other pleasing errors of young minds, is

the opinion of their own importance. He that has not yet remarked, how little attention his contemporaries can spare from their own affairs, conceives all eyes turned upon himself, and imagines every one that approaches him to be an enemy or a follower, an admirer or a spy.　He therefore considers his fame as involved in the event of every action. Many of the virtues and vices of youth proceed from this quick sense of reputation.　This it is that gives firmness and constancy, fidelity and disinterestedness, and it is this that kindles resentment for slight injuries, and dictates all the principles of sanguinary honour.

But as time brings him forward into the world, he soon discovers that he only shares fame or reproach with innumerable partners ; that he is left unmarked in the obscurity of the crowd ; and that what he does, whether good or bad, soon gives way to new objects of regard.　He then easily sets himself free from the anxieties of reputation, and considers praise or censure as a transient breach, which, while he hears it, is passing away, without any lasting mischief or advantage.

In youth, it is common to measure right and wrong by the opinion of the world, and, in age, to act without any measure but interest, and to lose shame without substituting virtue.

Such is the condition of life, that something is always wanting to happiness.　In youth, we have warm hopes, which are soon blasted by rashness and negligence, and great designs, which are defeated by inexperience.　In age, we have knowledge and prudence without spirit to exert, or motives to prompt them ; we are able to plan schemes, and regulate measures ; but have not time remaining to bring them to completion.[1]

1 Boswell quotes from "a small duodecimo volume, in which Johnson has written a variety of hints on different subjects," the following sketch of this number of *The Rambler*:—

" *Youth's Entry, &c.*

" Baxter's account of things in which he had changed his mind as he grew up. Voluminous.—No wonder.—If every man was to tell, or mark, on how many subjects he has changed, it would make vols. but the changes not always observed by man's self.—*F*rom pleasure to bus. [*business*] to quiet ; from thoughtfulness to reflect. to piety ; from dissipation to domestic. by impercept. gradat. but the change is certain. Dial *non progredi, progress. esse conspicimus.* Look back, consider what was thought at some dist. period.

"*Hope predom. in youth. Mind not willingly indulges unpleasing thoughts.* The world lies all enamelled before him, as a distant prospect sun-gilt ;—inequalities only found by coming to it. *Love is to be all joy—children excellent—F*ame to be constant—caresses of the great—applauses of the learned—smiles of Beauty.

" *Fear of disgrace—bashfulness—F*inds things of less importance. Miscarriages forgot like excellencies—if remembered, of no import. Danger of sinking into negligence of reputation. Lest the fear of disgrace destroy activity.

" *Confidence in himself.* Long tract of life before him.—No thought of sickness.—Embarrassment ot affairs.—Distraction of family. Public calamities.—No sense of the prevalence of bad habits. Negligent of time—ready to undertake—careless to pursue—all changed by time.

" *Confident of others*—unsuspecting as unexperienced—imagining himself secure against neglect, never imagines they will venture to treat him ill. Ready to trust ; expecting to be trusted. Convinced by time of the selfishness, the meanness, the cowardice, the treachery of men.

" Youth ambitious, as thinking honours easy to be had.

" Different kinds of praise pursued at different periods. Of the gay in youth.—dang. hurt, &c. despised.

No. 200. SATURDAY, FEBRUARY 15, 1752.

Nemo petit modicis quæ mittebantur amicis
A Seneca, quæ Piso bonus, quæ Cotta solebat
Largiri, namque et titulis et fascibus olim
Major habebatur donandi gloria ; solum
Poscimus ui cænes civiliter.   Hoc face, et esto
Esto, ut nunc multi, dives tibi, pauper amicis.—JUV.[1]

No man expects (for who so much a sot
Who has the times he lives in so forgot ?)
What Seneca, what Piso us'd to send,
To raise or to support a sinking friend.
Those godlike men, to wanting virtue kind,
Bounty well plac'd, preferr'd, and well design'd,
To all their titles, all that height of pow'r,
Which turns the brains of fools, and fools alone adore.
When your poor client is condemn'd t' attend,
'Tis all we ask, receive him as a friend :
Descend to this, and then we ask no more ;
Rich to yourself, to all beside be poor.—BOWLES.

" Of the fancy in manhood.   Ambit.—stocks—bargains.—
Of the wise and sober in old age—seriousness—formality
—maxims, but general—only of the rich, otherwise age is
happy—but at last everything referred to riches—no having
fame, honour, influence, without subjection to caprice.

" Horace [The motto is from Horace].

" Hard it would be if men entered life with the same views
with which they leave it, or left as they enter it.—No hope
—no undertaking—no regard to benevolence—no fear of
disgrace, &c.

" Youth to be taught the piety of age—age to retain the
honour of youth."—Boswell's *Johnson*, i. 205.

[1] Juvenal, *Satires*, v. 108.

To the RAMBLER.

MR. RAMBLER,

UCH is the tenderness or infirmity of many minds, that when any affliction oppresses them, they have immediate recourse to lamentation and complaint, which, though it can only be allowed reasonable when evils admit of remedy, and then only when addressed to those from whom the remedy is expected, yet seems even in hopeless and incurable distresses to be natural, since those by whom it is not indulged, imagine that they give a proof of extraordinary fortitude by suppressing it.

I am one of those who, with the Sancho of Cervantes, leave to higher characters the merit of suffering in silence, and give vent without scruple to any sorrow that swells in my heart[1] It is therefore to me a severe aggravation of a calamity, when it is such as in the common opinion will not justify the acerbity of exclamation, or support the

---

[1] "'Pray, sir,' said Sancho, 'sit a little more upright in your saddle ; for you seem to me to ride sideling, occasioned doubtless by your being so sorely bruised.' 'It is certainly so,' answered Don Quixote, 'and if I do not complain, it is because Knights-errant are not allowed to complain of any wound whatever, even though their entrails should come out of the body.' 'If that be the case, I have nothing to reply,' answered Sancho ; 'but God knows I should be glad to hear your worship complain when anything ails you. As for myself, I shall be apt to complain of the least pain I feel, unless this business of not complaining be understood to extend to the squires as well as the knights."—*Don Quixote*, bk i., ch. viii.

solemnity of vocal grief. Yet many pains are incident to a man of delicacy, which the unfeeling world cannot be persuaded to pity, and which, when they are separated from their peculiar and personal circumstances, will never be considered as important enough to claim attention, or deserve redress.

Of this kind will appear to gross and vulgar apprehensions, the miseries which I endured in a morning visit to Prospero,[1] a man lately raised to wealth by a lucky project, and too much intoxicated by sudden elevation, or too little polished by thought and conversation, to enjoy his present fortune with elegance and decency.

We set out in the world together[2]; and for a long time mutually assisted each other in our exigencies, as either happened to have money or influence beyond his immediate necessities. You know that nothing generally endears men so

[1] "Some of the characters in *The Rambler* are believed to have been actually drawn from the life, particularly that of Prospero from Garrick, who never entirely forgave its pointed satire."—Boswell's *Johnson*, i. 216.

[2] "Both Johnson and Garrick used to talk pleasantly of their first journey to London. Garrick, evidently meaning to embellish a little, said one day in my hearing, 'We rode and tied.' And the Bishop of Killaloe informed me, that at another time, when Johnson and Garrick were dining together in a pretty large company, Johnson humorously ascertaining the chronology of something, expressed himself thus:—'That was the year when I came to London with twopence halfpenny in my pocket.' Garrick overhearing him, exclaimed, 'Eh? What do you say? With twopence halfpenny in your pocket?' Johnson. 'Why, yes; when I came with twopence halfpenny in *my* pocket, and thou, Davy, with three-halfpence in thine.'"—*Ib.*, i. 101.

much as participation of dangers and misfortunes;
I therefore always considered Prospero as united
with me in the strongest league of kindness, and
imagined that our friendship was only to be
broken by the hand of death. I felt at his sudden
shoot of success[1] an honest and disinterested joy;
but as I want no part of his superfluities, am not
willing to descend from that equality in which we
hitherto have lived.

Our intimacy was regarded by me as a dispensa-
tion from ceremonial visits; and it was so long
before I saw him at his new house, that he gently
complained of my neglect, and obliged me to
come on a day appointed. I kept my promise,
but found that the impatience of my friend arose
not from any desire to communicate his happiness,
but to enjoy his superiority.

When I told my name at the door, the footman went to see if his master was at home, and,
by the tardiness of his return, gave me reason to
suspect that time was taken to deliberate. He
then informed me, that Prospero desired my company, and showed the staircase carefully secured
by mats from the pollution of my feet. The best
apartments were ostentatiously set open, that I
might have a distant view of the magnificence
which I was not permitted to approach; and my
old friend receiving me with all the insolence of
condescension at the top of the stairs, conducted

---

1 Gray, writing in the end of 1741 or early in 1742, says:
—"Did I tell you about Mr. Garrick, that the town are
horn-mad after: there are a dozen dukes of a night at Good-
man's *Fields* sometimes."—Gray's *Works*, ed. 1858, ii. 185.

me to a back room, where he told me he always breakfasted when he had not great company.

On the floor where we sat, lay a carpet covered with a cloth, of which Prospero ordered his servant to lift up a corner, that I might contemplate the brightness of the colours, and the elegance of the texture, and asked me whether I had ever seen any thing so fine before? I did not gratify his folly with any outcries of admiration, but coldly bade the footman let down the cloth.

We then sat down, and I began to hope that pride was glutted with persecution, when Prospero desired that I would give the servant leave to adjust the cover of my chair, which was slipt a little aside, to show the damask ; he informed me that he had bespoke ordinary chairs for common use, but had been disappointed by his tradesman. I put the chair aside with my foot, and drew another so hastily, that I was entreated not to rumple the carpet.

Breakfast was at last set, and as I was not willing to indulge the peevishness that began to seize me, I commended the tea[1] ; Prospero then told me, that another time I should taste his finest sort, but that he had only a very small quantity remaining, and reserved it for those

[1] "Dr. SCOTT. 'Garrick has been represented as very saving.' JOHNSON. 'With his domestic saving we have nothing to do. I remember drinking tea with him long ago, when Peg Woffington made it, and he grumbled at her for making it too strong.' When Johnson told this little anecdote to Sir Joshua Reynolds, he mentioned a circumstance which he omitted to-day :—'Why (said Garrick) it is as red as blood.' "—Boswell's *Johnson*, iii. 264.

whom he thought himself obliged to treat with
particular respect[1].

While we were conversing upon such subjects
as imagination happened to suggest, he frequently
digressed into directions to the servant that
waited, or made a slight inquiry after the jeweller
or silversmith ; and once, as I was pursuing an
argument with some degree of earnestness, he
started from his posture of attention, and ordered,
that if Lord Lofty called on him that morning, he
should be shown into the best parlour.[2]

[1] Out of this passage no doubt grew the following story,
recorded in C. C. Greville's *Journal*, ed. 1874, ii. 316. "Lord
Holland told some stories of Johnson and Garrick which he
had heard from Kemble. . . . When Garrick was in the zenith
of his popularity and grown rich, and lived with the great,
and while Johnson was yet obscure, the Doctor [Johnson was
not a Doctor in those days] used to drink tea with him, and
he would say, 'Davy, I do not envy you your money nor
your fine acquaintance, but I envy you your power of drinking such tea as this.' 'Yes,' said Garrick, 'it is very good
tea ; but it is not my best, nor that which I give to my Lord
this, and Sir somebody t'other.'"

[2] "Johnson could not patiently endure to hear that such
respect as he thought due only to higher intellectual qualities
should be bestowed on men of slighter, though perhaps more
amusing, talents. I told him that one morning when I went
to breakfast with Garrick, who was very vain of his intimacy with Lord Camden, he accosted me thus: 'Pray now,
did you—did you meet a little lawyer turning the corner,
eh?' 'No, sir,' said I ; 'pray what do you mean by the
question?' 'Why,' replied Garrick, with an affected indifference, yet as if standing on tip-toe, 'Lord Camden has
this moment left me. We have had a long walk together.'
JOHNSON. 'Well, sir, Garrick talked very properly. Lord
Camden *was* a *little lawyer* to be associating so familiarly
with a player.'"—Boswell's *Johnson*, iii. 311.

My patience was yet not wholly subdued. I was willing to promote his satisfaction, and therefore observed that the figures on the china, were eminently pretty. Prospero had now an opportunity of calling for his Dresden china, which, says he, I always associate with my chased tea-kettle. The cups were brought ; I once resolved not to have looked upon them, but my curiosity prevailed. When I had examined them a little, Prospero desired me to set them down, for they who were accustomed only to common dishes, seldom handled china with much care. You will, I hope, commend my philosophy, when I tell you that I did not dash his baubles to the ground.

He was now so much elevated with his own greatness, that he thought some humility necessary to avert the glance of envy, and therefore told me, with an air of soft composure, that I was not to estimate life by external appearance, that all these shining acquisitions had added little to his happiness, that he still remembered with pleasure the days in which he and I were upon the level, and had often, in the moment of reflection, been doubtful, whether he should lose much by changing his condition for mine.

I began now to be afraid lest his pride should, by silence and submission, be emboldened to insults that could not easily be borne, and therefore coolly considered, how I should repress it without such bitterness of reproof as I was yet unwilling to use. But he interrupted my meditation, by asking leave to be dressed, and told me, that he had promised to attend some ladies in the park, and, if I was going the same way, would take me in his chariot. I had no inclination to any other favours, and therefore left him without any intention of seeing him again, unless some misfortune should restore his understanding.

I am, &c.

ASPER.

Though I am not wholly insensible of the provocations which my correspondent has received, I cannot altogether commend the keenness of his resentment, nor encourage him to persist in his resolution of breaking off all commerce with his old acquaintance. One of the golden precepts of Pythagoras directs, that *a ɔfriend should not be hated for little ɔfaults;* and surely he, upon whom nothing worse can be charged, than that he mats his stairs, and covers his carpet, and sets out his finery to show before those whom he does not admit to use it, has yet committed nothing that should exclude him from common degrees of kindness. Such improprieties often proceed rather from stupidity than malice. Those who thus shine only to dazzle, are influenced merely by custom and example, and neither examine, nor are qualified to examine, the motives cf their own practice, or to state the nice limits between elegance and ostentation. They are often innocent of the pain which their vanity produces, and insult others when they have no worse purpose than to please themselves.

He that too much refines his delicacy will always endanger his quiet. Of those with whom

nature and virtue oblige us to converse, some are
ignorant of the art of pleasing, and offend when
they design to caress ; some are negligent, and
gratify themselves without regard to the quiet of
another ; some, perhaps, are malicious, and feel
no greater satisfaction in prosperity, than that of
raising envy and trampling inferiority. But whatever be the motive of insult, it is always best to
overlook it, for folly scarcely can deserve resentment, and malice is punished by neglect.

No. 202. SATURDAY, FEBRUARY 22, 1752.

Πρὸς ἄπαντα δειλὸς ἐστὶν ὁ πένης πράγματα
Καὶ πάντας αὐτὸν καταφρονεῖν ὑπολαμβάνει.
'Ο δὲ μετρίως πράττων περισκελέστερον
Ἄπαντα τ᾽ ἀνιαρὰ, Δαμπρία, φέρει.—CALLIMACHUS.

From no affliction is the poor exempt,
He thinks each eye surveys him with contempt,
Unmanly poverty subdues the heart,
Cankers each wound, and sharpens ev'ry dart.
—F. LEWIS.

AMONG those who have endeavoured to
promote learning, and rectify judgment, it has been long customary to
complain of the abuse of words which
are often admitted to signify things so different,
that, instead of assisting the understanding as
vehicles of knowledge, they produce error, dissen-
sion, and perplexity, because what is affirmed in
one sense, is received in another.

If this ambiguity sometimes embarrasses the most solemn controversies, and obscures the demonstrations of science, it may be well expected to infest the pompous periods of declaimers, whose purpose is often only to amuse with fallacies, and change the colours of truth and falsehood ; or the musical compositions of poets, whose style is professedly figurative, and whose art is imagined to consist in distorting words from their original meaning.

There are few words of which the reader believes himself better to know the import, than of *poverty ;* yet, whoever studies either the poets or philosophers, will find such an account of the condition expressed by that term as his experience or observation will not easily discover to be true. Instead of the meanness, distress, complaint, anxiety, and dependence, which have hitherto been combined in his ideas of poverty, he will read of content, innocence, and cheerfulness, of health and safety, tranquillity and freedom ; of pleasures not known but to men unencumbered with possessions ; and of sleep that sheds his balsamic anodynes only on the cottage. Such are the blessings to be obtained by the resignation of riches, that kings might descend from their thrones, and generals retire from a triumph, only to slumber undisturbed in the elysium of poverty.[1]

---

[1] "Why rather, sleep, liest thou in smoky cribs
Upon uneasy pallets stretching thee,
And hush'd with buzzing night-flies to thy slumber,
Than in the perfumed chambers of the great," &c.
—*Henry IV.* Second Part, Act iii. sc. i., l. 9.

If these authors do not deceive us, nothing can be more absurd than that perpetual contest for wealth which keeps the world in commotion ; nor any complaints more justly censured than those which proceed from want of the gifts of fortune, which we are taught by the great masters of moral wisdom to consider as golden shackles, by which the wearer is at once disabled and adorned ; as luscious poisons which may for a time please the palate, but soon betray their malignity by languor and by pain.

It is the great privilege of poverty to be happy unenvied, to be healthful without physic, and secure without a guard ; to obtain from the bounty of nature what the great and wealthy are compelled to procure by the help of artists and attendants, of flatterers and spies.[1]

But it will be found upon a nearer view, that they who extol the happiness of poverty, do not mean the same state with those who deplore its miseries.   Poets have their imaginations filled with ideas of magnificence ; and being accustomed to contemplate the downfall of empires, or to contrive forms of lamentations for monarchs in distress, rank all the classes of mankind in a state of poverty, who make no approaches to the dignity of

[1] Boswell describes how he and Johnson entered a hut in the Island of Col :—"There was but one bed for all the family, and the hut was very smoky.   When he came out he said to me, 'Et hoc secundum sententiam philosophorum est esse beatus.'   BOSWELL. 'The philosophers, when they placed happiness in a cottage, supposed cleanliness and no smoke.' JOHNSON. 'Sir, they did not think about either.'"—Boswell's *Johnson*, v. 293.

crowns. To be poor, in the epic language, is only not to command the wealth of nations, nor to have fleets and armies in pay.

Vanity has perhaps contributed to this impropriety of style. He that wishes to become a philosopher at a cheap rate, easily gratifies his ambition by submitting to poverty when he does not feel it, and by boasting his contempt of riches, when he has already more than he enjoys. He who would show the extent of his views, and grandeur of his conceptions, or discover his acquaintance with splendour and magnificence, may talk like Cowley, of an humble station and quiet obscurity, of the paucity of nature's wants, and the inconveniencies of superfluity, and at last, like him, limit his desires to five hundred pounds a year[1] ; a fortune, indeed, not exuberant, when we compare it with the expences of pride and luxury, but to which it little becomes a philosopher to affix the name of poverty, since no man can, with any propriety, be termed

[1] "When you have pared away all the vanity, what solid and natural contentment does there remain which may not be had with five hundred pounds a year?"—Cowley's *Works*, ed. 1674, last part, p. 123. In the beginning of the same essay he says :—

> "If ever I more riches did desire
> Than cleanliness and quiet do require,
> If e'er ambition did my fancy cheat
> With any wish so mean as to be great,
> Continue, Heav'n, still from me to remove
> The humble blessings of that life I love."

Johnson, in the last year of his life, said that if his pension were doubled, so that he should receive six hundred pounds a year, "he would have the consciousness that he should pass the remainder of his life in splendour."—Boswell's *Johnson*, iv. 337.

poor, who does not see the greater part of mankind richer than himself.

As little is the general condition of human life understood by the panegyrists and historians, who amuse us with accounts of the poverty of heroes and sages. Riches are of no value in themselves, their use is discovered only in that which they procure. They are not coveted, unless by narrow understandings, which confound the means with the end, but for the sake of power, influence, and esteem ; or, by some of less elevated and refined sentiments, as necessary to sensual enjoyment.

The pleasures of luxury many have, without uncommon virtue, been able to despise, even when affluence and idleness have concurred to tempt them ; and therefore he who feels nothing from indigence but the want of gratifications which he could not in any other condition make consistent with innocence, has given no proof of eminent patience. Esteem and influence every man desires, but they are equally pleasing, and equally valuable, by whatever means they are obtained ; and whoever has found the art of securing them without the help of money, ought, in reality, to be accounted rich, since he has all that riches can purchase to a wise man. Cincinnatus, though he lived upon a few acres cultivated by his own hand, was sufficiently removed from all the evils generally comprehended under the name of poverty, when his reputation was such that the voice of his country called him from his farm to take absolute command into his hand ; nor was Diogenes much mortified by his residence in a tub, where he was honoured with the visit of Alexander the Great.

The same fallacy has conciliated veneration to the religious orders. When we behold a man abdicating the hope of terrestrial possessions, and precluding himself, by an irrevocable vow, from the pursuit and acquisition of all that his fellow-beings consider as worthy of wishes and endeavours, we are immediately struck with the purity, abstraction, and firmness of his mind, and regard him as wholly employed in securing the interests of futurity, and devoid of any other care than to gain at whatever price the surest passage to eternal rest.

Yet, what can the votary be justly said to have lost of his present happiness? If he resides in a convent, he converses only with men whose condition is the same with his own ; he has, from the munificence of the founder, all the necessaries of life, and is safe from that "destitution which Hooker declares to be such an impediment to virtue, as, till it be removed, suffereth not the mind of man to admit any other care." All temptations to envy and competition are shut out from his retreat ; he is not pained with the sight of unattainable dignity, nor insulted with the bluster of insolence, or the smile of forced familiarity. If he wanders abroad, the sanctity of his character amply compensates all other distinctions ; he is seldom seen but with reverence, nor heard but with submission.

It has been remarked that death, though often defied in the field, seldom fails to terrify when it approaches the bed of sickness in its natural horror ;[1] so poverty may easily be endured, while associated with dignity and reputation, but will always be shunned and dreaded, when it is accompanied with ignominy and contempt.

No. 203. TUESDAY, FEBRUARY 25, 1752.

Quum volet illa dies, quæ nil nisi corporis hujus
Jus habet, incerti spatium mihi finiat ævi.—OVID.[2]

Come, soon or late, death's undetermin'd day,
This mortal being only can decay.—WELSTED.

IT seems to be the fate of man to seek all his consolations in futurity. The time present is seldom able to fill desire or imagination with immediate enjoyment, and we are forced to supply its deficiencies by recollection or anticipation.

Every one has so often detected the fallaciousness of hope, and the inconvenience of teaching himself to expect what a thousand accidents may preclude, that, when time has abated the confidence with which youth rushes out to take possession of the world, we endeavour, or wish, to find entertainment in the review of life, and to repose

---

1 " Or i'ay pensé souvent d'où venoit cela, qu'aux guerres le visage de la mort, soit que nous la veoyions en nous ou en aultruy, nous semble sans comparaison moins effroyable qu'en nos maisons (aultrement ceseroit une armee de medecins et de pleurars)."—*Essais de Montaigne*, i. 19.

2 *Metamorphoses*, xv. 873.

upon real facts, and certain experience. This is perhaps one reason, among many, why age delights in narratives.

But so full is the world of calamity, that every source of pleasure is polluted, and every retirement of tranquillity disturbed. When time has supplied us with events sufficient to employ our thoughts, it has mingled them with so many disasters, that we shrink from their remembrance, dread their intrusion upon our minds, and fly from them as from enemies that pursue us with torture.

No man past the middle point of life can sit down to feast upon the pleasures of youth without finding the banquet embittered by the cup of sorrow ; he may revive lucky accidents and pleasing extravagancies ; many days of harmless frolic, or nights of honest festivity, will perhaps recur ; or, if he has been engaged in scenes of action, and acquainted with affairs of difficulty and vicissitudes of fortune, he may enjoy the nobler pleasure of looking back upon distress firmly supported, dangers resolutely encountered, and opposition artfully defeated. Æneas properly comforts his companions, when, after the horrors of a storm, they have landed on an unknown and desolate country, with the hope that their miseries will be at some distant time recounted with delight.[1] There are few higher gratifications than that of reflection on surmounted evils, when they were not incurred nor protracted by our fault, and neither reproach us with cowardice nor guilt.

[1] " ——forsan et hæc olim meminisse juvabit."
                                        —Æneid, i. 203.

But this felicity is almost always abated by the reflection that they with whom we should be most pleased to share it are now in the grave. A few years make such havoc in human generations, that we soon see ourselves deprived of those with whom we entered the world, and whom the participation of pleasures or fatigues had endeared to our remembrance. The man of enterprise recounts his adventures and expedients, but is forced, at the close of the relation, to pay a sigh to the names of those that contributed to his success ; he that passes his life among the gayer part of mankind, has his remembrance stored with remarks and repartees of wits, whose sprightliness and merriment are now lost in perpetual silence ; the trader, whose industry has supplied the want of inheritance, repines in solitary plenty at the absence of companions, with whom he had planned out amusements for his latter years ; and the scholar, whose merit, after a long series of efforts, raises him from obscurity, looks round in vain from his exaltation for his old friends or enemies, whose applause or mortification would heighten his triumph.

Among Martial's requisites to happiness is, *Res non parta labore, sed relicta*[1], an estate not gained by industry, but left by inheritance. It is necessary to the completion of every good, that it be timely obtained ; for whatever comes at the

---

[1] " Vitam quæ faciant beatiorem,
    Jucundissime Martialis, hæc sunt :
    Res non parta labore, sed relicta," &c.
                              —Martial, x. 47.

close of life will come too late to give much
delight[1] ; yet all human happiness has its defects.
Of what we do not gain for ourselves we have
only a faint and imperfect fruition, because we
cannot compare the difference between want and
possession, or at least can derive from it no conviction of our own abilities, nor any increase
of self-esteem ; what we acquire by bravery or
science, by mental or corporal diligence, comes at
last when we cannot communicate, and therefore
cannot enjoy it.

Thus every period of life is obliged to borrow
its happiness from the time to come. In youth
we have nothing past to entertain us, and in age,
we derive little from retrospect but hopeless
sorrow. Yet the future likewise has its limits,
which the imagination dreads to approach, but
which we see to be not far distant. The loss
of our friends and companions impresses hourly
upon us the necessity of our own departure ; we
know that the schemes of man are quickly at an
end, that we must soon lie down in the grave
with the forgotten multitudes of former ages, and
yield our place to others, who, like us, shall be
driven a while by hope or fear, about the surface
of the earth, and then like us be lost in the shades
of death.

[1] Johnson wrote this *Rambler* when his wife was on her
death-bed. Three years later, in his letter to Lord Chesterfield, he says :—" The notice which you have been pleased to
take of my labours, had it been early, had been kind ; but it
has been delayed till I am indifferent, and cannot enjoy it ;
till I am solitary, and cannot impart it ; till I am known,
and do not want it."—Boswell's *Johnson*, i. 262.

Beyond this termination of our material existence, we are therefore obliged to extend our
hopes ; and almost every man indulges his
imagination with something, which is not to
happen till he has changed his manner of being ;
some amuse themselves with entails and settle-
ments, provide for the perpetuation of families
and honours, or contrive to obviate the dissipation of the fortunes, which it has been their
business to accumulate ; others, more refined or
exalted, congratulate their own hearts upon the
future extent of their reputation, the reverence of
distant nations, and the gratitude of unprejudiced
posterity.

They whose souls are so chained down to
coffers and tenements, that they cannot conceive
a state in which they shall look upon them with
less solicitude, are seldom attentive or flexible to
arguments ; but the votaries of fame are capable
of reflection, and therefore may be called to re-
consider the probability of their expectations.

Whether to be remembered in remote times be
worthy of a wise man's wish, has not yet been
satisfactorily decided ; and, indeed, to be long
remembered, can happen to so small a number,
that the bulk of mankind has very little interest
in the question. There is never room in the
world for more than a certain quantity or measure
of renown.[1] The necessary business of life, the

1 "Sir Joshua Reynolds said that Goldsmith considered
fame as one great parcel, to the whole of which he laid claim,
and whoever partook of any part of it, whether dancer,
singer, sleight of hand man, or tumbler, deprived him of his
right."—Northcote's *Life of Reynolds,* i. 248.

immediate pleasures or pains of every condition, leave us not leisure beyond a fixed proportion for contemplations which do not forcibly influence our present welfare. When this vacuity is filled, no characters can be admitted into the circulation of fame, but by occupying the place of some that must be thrust into oblivion. The eye of the mind, like that of the body, can only extend its view to new objects, by losing sight of those which are now before it.

Reputation is therefore a meteor, which blazes a while and disappears for ever ; and, if we except a few transcendent and invincible names, which no revolutions of opinion or length of time is able to suppress ; all those that engage our thoughts, or diversify our conversation, are every moment hasting to obscurity, as new favourites are adopted by fashion.

It is not therefore from this world, that any ray of comfort can proceed, to cheer the gloom of the last hour. But futurity has still its prospects ; there is yet happiness in reserve, which, if we transfer our attention to it, will support us in the pains of disease, and the languor of decay. This happiness we may expect with confidence, because it is out of the power of chance, and may be attained by all that sincerely desire and earnestly pursue it. On this therefore every mind ought finally to rest. Hope is the chief blessing of man, and that hope only is rational, of which we are certain that it cannot deceive us.

No. 208. SATURDAY, MARCH, 14,[1] 1752.

' Ἡράκλειτος ἐγώ· τί με ὦ κάτω ἕλκετ᾽ ἄμουσοι;
Οὐχ᾽ ὑμῖν ἐπόνουν, τοῖς δέ μ᾽ ἐπισταμένοις·
Εἷς ἐμοὶ ἄνθρωπος τρισμύριοι· οἱ δ᾽ ἀνάριθμοι
Οὐδείς· ταῦτ᾽ αὐδῶ καὶ Παρὰ Περσεφόνῃ.
                                    —Diog. Laert.

Begone, ye blockheads, Heraclitus cries,
And leave my labours to the learn'd and wise ;
By wit, by knowledge, studious to be read,
I scorn the multitude, alive and dead.

TIME, which puts an end to all human pleasures and sorrows, has likewise concluded the labours of the Rambler. Having supported, for two years, the anxious employment of a periodical writer, and multiplied my essays to upwards of two hundred, I have now determined to desist.

The reasons of this resolution it is of little importance to declare, since justification is unnecessary when no objection is made. I am far from supposing that the cessation of my performances will raise any inquiry, for I have never been much a favourite of the public, nor can boast, that, in the progress of my undertaking, I have been animated by the rewards of the liberal, the caresses of the great, or the praises of the eminent.

[1] In the first edition the date is wrongly given as March 17 —the day of Mrs. Johnson's death.

But I have no design to gratify pride by sub-mission, or malice by lamentation; nor think it reasonable to complain of neglect from those whose regard I never solicited. If I have not been distinguished by the distributors of literary honours, I have seldom descended to the arts by which favour is obtained. I have seen the meteors of fashion rise and fall, without any attempt to add a moment to their duration. I have never complied with ˌtemporary curiosity, nor enabled my readers to discuss the topic of the day; I have rarely exemplified my assertions by living charac-ters; in my papers no man could look for censures of his enemies, or praises of himself; and they only were expected to peruse them whose passions left them leisure for abstracted truth, and whom virtue could please by its naked dignity.

To some, however, I am indebted for encourage-ment, and to others for assistance. The number of my friends was never great, but they have been such as would not suffer me to think that I was writing in vain, and I did not feel much dejection from the want of popularity.

My obligations having not been frequent, my acknowledgments may be soon despatched. I can restore to all my correspondents their pro-ductions with little diminution of the bulk of my volumes, though not without the loss of some pieces to which particular honours have been paid.

The parts from which I claim no other praise than that of having given them an opportunity of appearing, are the four billets in the tenth paper, the second letter in the fifteenth, the thirtieth, the forty-fourth, the ninety-seventh, and the hundredth papers, and the second letter in the hundred and seventh.[1]

Having thus deprived myself of many excuses which candour might have admitted for the inequality of my compositions, being no longer able to allege the necessity of gratifying correspondents, the importunity with which publication was solicited, or obstinacy with which correction was rejected, I must remain accountable for all my faults, and submit, without subterfuge, to the censures of criticism, which, however, I shall not endeavour to soften by a formal deprecation, or to overbear by the influence of a patron. The supplications of an author never yet reprieved him a moment from oblivion ; and, though greatness has sometimes sheltered guilt, it can afford no protection to ignorance or dulness. Having hitherto attempted only the propagation of truth, I will not at last violate it by the confession of terrors which I do not feel ; having laboured to maintain the dignity of virtue, I will not now degrade it by the meanness of dedication.[2]

The seeming vanity with which I have some-

1 The contributors were Miss Mulso (afterwards Mrs. Chapone), Miss Catherine Talbot, Miss Carter, and Samuel Richardson. Johnson, in the Preface to Richardson's *Rambler* (No. 97), describes him as "an author from whom the age has received greater favours, who has enlarged the knowledge of human nature, and taught the passions to move at the command of virtue."

2 "Though the loftiness of Dr. Johnson's mind prevented him from ever dedicating in his own person, he wrote a very great number of dedications for others."—Boswell's *Johnson,* ii. i.

times spoken of myself, would perhaps require an
apology, were it not extenuated by the example of
those who have published essays before me, and
by the privilege which every nameless writer has
been hitherto allowed. "A mask," says Castiglione, " confers a right of acting and speaking with
" less restraint, even when the wearer happens to
" be known."[1]   He that is discovered without his
own consent, may claim some indulgence, and cannot be rigorously called to justify those sallies or
frolics which his disguise must prove him desirous
to conceal.[2]

But I have been cautious lest this offence should
be frequently or grossly committed ; for, as one of
the philosophers directs us to live with a friend as
with one that is some time to become an enemy, I
have always thought it the duty of an anonymous
author to write as if he expected to be hereafter
known.

I am willing to flatter myself with hopes, that,
by collecting these papers, I am not preparing for
my future life, either shame or repentance.   That
all are happily imagined, or accurately polished,

[1] "Johnson said, 'The best book that ever was written
upon good breeding, *Il Corteggiano*, by Castiglione, grew up
at the little court of Urbino, and you should read it.'"—Boswell's *Johnson*, v. 276.   Castiglione was born in 1478 and
died in 1529.   The passage which Johnson quotes from
memory is found in bk. ii., p. 19, of the English translation,
entitled *The Courtier*, ed. 1724.

[2] Edward Cave, the publisher of *The Rambler*, says that
" Garrick and others, who knew the author's powers and style
from the first, unadvisedly asserting their suspicions, over-
turned the scheme of secrecy."—Boswell's *Johnson*, i. 209,
note 1.

that the same sentiments have not sometimes re-
curred, or the same expressions been too frequently
repeated, I have not confidence in my abilities
sufficient to warrant. He that condemns himself
to compose on a stated day, will often bring to his
task an attention dissipated, a memory embarrassed, an imagination overwhelmed, a mind distracted with anxieties, a body languishing with
disease ; he will labour on a barren topic till it is
too late to change it ; or, in the ardour of invention, diffuse his thoughts into wild exuberance,
which the pressing hour of publication cannot
suffer judgment to examine or reduce.

Whatever shall be the final sentence of mankind, I have at least endeavoured to deserve
their kindness. I have laboured to refine our
language to grammatical purity, and to clear it
from colloquial barbarisms, licentious idioms, and
irregular combinations. Something, perhaps, I
have added to the elegance of its construction,
and something to the harmony of its cadence.[1]
When common words were less pleasing to the
ear, or less distinct in their signification, I have
familiarised the terms of philosophy, by applying
them to popular ideas, but have rarely admitted
any word not authorised by former writers ;[2]

[1] "Sir William Temple (said Johnson) was the first
writer who gave cadence to English prose."—Boswell's *Johnson*, iii. 257.

    "Enfin Malherbe vint, et le premier en France
    Fit sentir dans les vers une juste cadence,
    D'un mot mis en sa place enseigna le pouvoir."
        —*Œuvres de Voltaire*, ed. 1819-25, xlii. 10.

[2] See *ante*, p. 53, n. 1.

for I believe that whoever knows the English tongue, in its present extent, will be able to express his thoughts without further help from other nations.[1]

As it has been my principal design to inculcate wisdom or piety, I have allotted few papers to the idle sports of imagination. Some, perhaps, may be found, of which the highest excellence is harmless merriment; but scarcely any man is so steadily serious as not to complain, that the severity of dictatorial instruction has been too seldom relieved, and that he is driven by the sternness of the Rambler's philosophy to more cheerful and airy companions.[2]

Next to the excursions of fancy are the disquisitions of criticism, which, in my opinion, is only to be ranked among the subordinate and instrumental arts. Arbitrary decision and general exclamation I have carefully avoided, by asserting nothing without a reason, and establishing all my principles of judgment on unalterable and evident truth.

In the pictures of life I have never been so studious of novelty or surprise, as to depart wholly from all resemblance; a fault which writers deservedly celebrated frequently commit, that they may raise, as the occasion requires, either

[1] See Boswell's *Johnson*, iii. 343 for Johnson's definition of *transpire*—"To escape from secrecy to notice; a sense lately innovated from *France*, without necessity."

[2] "No periodical author who always maintains his gravity and does not sometimes sacrifice to the graces, must expect to keep in vogue for any considerable time."—Addison, *The Freeholder*, No. 45.

mirth or abhorrence. Some enlargement may be
allowed to declamation, and some exaggeration to
burlesque ; but as they deviate farther from reality,
they become less useful, because their lessons will
fail of application. The mind of the reader is
carried away from the contemplation of his own
manners ; he finds in himself no likeness to the
phantom before him ; and though he laughs or
rages, is not reformed.

The essays professedly serious, if I have been
able to execute my own intentions, will be found
exactly conformable to the precepts of Christianity, without any accommodation to the licentiousness and levity of the present age. I therefore
look back on this part of my work with pleasure,
which no blame or praise of man shall diminish
or augment.[1] I shall never envy the honours
which wit and learning obtain in any other cause,
if I can be numbered among the writers who
have given ardour to virtue, and confidence to
truth.[2]

Αὐτῶν ἐκ μακάρων ἀντάξιος εἴη ἀμοιβή.[3]

Celestial pow'rs ! that piety regard,
From You my labours wait their last reward.

[1] "The real satisfaction which praise can afford is by re-
peating aloud the whispers of conscience, and by showing us
that we have not endeavoured to deserve well in vain."—
Rambler, No. 136.

[2] The last line in this paragraph Colonel Myddelton, of
Gwaynynog, near Denbigh, inscribed on an urn which he
set up "on the banks of a rivulet in his park, where Johnson
delighted to stand and repeat verses."—Boswell's *Johnson*,
iv. 421.

[3] Dr. Parr, who wrote the ponderous inscription on

Johnson's monument in St. Paul's Cathedral, says:—
"After I had written the epitaph Sir Joshua Reynolds
told me there was a scroll. I was in a rage. A scroll.
Why, Ned, this is vile modern contrivance. I wanted one
train of ideas. What could I do with the scroll? Johnson
held it, and Johnson must speak in it. . . . Mr.
Seward, hearing of my difficulty, and no scholar, suggested
the closing line in *The Rambler;* had I looked there I
should have anticipated the suggestion. It is the closing
line in Dionysius's *Periegesis.* I adopted it and gave Seward
the praise. 'Oh,' quoth Sir William Scott, 'μακάρων is
Heathenish, and the Dean and Chapter will hesitate.' 'The
more fools they,' said I. But to prevent disputes I have
altered it:—

'Εν μακάρεσσι πόνων ἀντάξιος εἴη ἀμοιβη."

—Boswell's *Johnson,* iv. 445.

THE ADVENTURER.

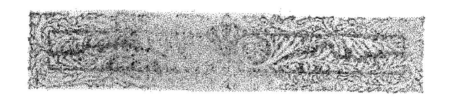

THE ADVENTURER

... Tollere humo ...

On eagle's wing to pant of praise I go,
And leave the gazing multitude below.

No. 69. TUESDAY, JULY 3, 1753.

Ferè libenter homines id quod volunt credunt.—CÆSAR.[2]
Men willingly believe what they wish to be true.

TULLY has long ago observed, that no man, however weakened by long life, is so conscious of his own decrepitude, as not to imagine that he may yet hold his station in the world for another year.[3]

Of the truth of this remark every day furnishes new confirmation: there is no part of life, in which men for the most part are less to expect the stroke of death, than when every other eye

---

[1] *Georgics,* iii. 8.
[2] *Gallic War,* iii. 18.
[3] "Nemo enim est tam senex qui se annum non putet posse vivere."—*De Senectute,* vii. 24.

THE ADVENTURER.

Tentanda via est ; qua me quoque possim
Tollere humo, victorque virum volitare per ora.—VIRGIL.[1]
On vent'rous wing in quest of praise I go,
And leave the gazing multitude below.

No. 69. TUESDAY, JULY 3, 1753.

Ferè libenter homines id quod volunt credunt.—CÆSAR.[2]
Men willingly believe what they wish to be true.

TULLY has long ago observed, that no man, however weakened by long life, is so conscious of his own decrepitude, as not to imagine that he may yet hold his station in the world for another year.[3]

Of the truth of this remark every day furnishes new confirmation : there is no time of life, in which men for the most part seem less to expect the stroke of death, than when every other eye

[1] *Georgics*, iii. 8.
[2] *Gallic War*, iii. 18.
[3] "Nemo enim est tam senex qui se annum non putet posse vivere."—*De Senectute*, vii. 24.

sees it impending ; or are more busy in providing for another year than when it is plain to all but themselves, that at another year they cannot arrive. Though every funeral that passes before their eyes evinces the deceitfulness of such expectations, since every man who is borne to the grave thought himself equally certain of living at least to the next year ; the survivor still continues to flatter himself, and is never at a loss for some reason why his life should be protracted, and the voracity of death continue to be pacified with some other prey.

But this is only one of the innumerable artifices practised in the universal conspiracy of mankind against themselves : every age and every condition indulges some darling fallacy ; every man amuses himself with projects which he knows to be improbable, and which, therefore, he resolves to pursue without daring to examine them. Whatever any man ardently desires, he very readily believes that he shall some time attain : he whose intemperance has overwhelmed him with diseases, while he languishes in the spring, expects vigour and recovery from the summer sun ; and while he melts away in the summer, transfers his hopes to the frosts of winter : he that gazes upon elegance or pleasure, which want of money hinders him from imitating or partaking, comforts himself that the time of distress will soon be at an end, and that every day brings him nearer to a state of happiness ; though he knows it has passed not only without acquisition of advantage, but perhaps without endeavours after it, in the formation of schemes that cannot be executed, and in the contemplation of prospects that cannot be approached.

Such is the general dream in which we all slumber out our time : every man thinks the day coming, in which he shall be gratified with all his wishes, in which he shall leave all those competitors behind, who are now rejoicing like himself in the expectation of victory ; the day is always coming to the servile in which they shall be powerful, to the obscure in which they shall be eminent, and to the deformed in which they shall be beautiful.

If any of my readers has looked with so little attention on the world about him, as to imagine this representation exaggerated beyond probability, let him reflect a little upon his own life ; let him consider what were his hopes and prospects ten years ago, and what additions he then expected to be made by ten years to his happiness : those years are now elapsed ; have they made good the promise that was extorted from them, have they advanced his fortune, enlarged his knowledge, or reformed his conduct, to the degree that was once expected ? I am afraid, every man that recollects his hopes, must confess his disappointment ; and own that day has glided unprofitably after day, and that he is still at the same distance from the point of happiness.

With what consolations can those, who have thus miscarried in their chief design, elude the memory of their ill success ? with what amusements can they pacify their discontent, after the loss of so large a portion of life ? they can give themselves up again to the same delusions, they can form new schemes of airy gratifications, and fix another period of felicity ; they can again resolve to trust the promise which they know will be broken, they can walk in a circle with their eyes shut, and persuade themselves to think that they go forward.

Of every great and complicated event, part depends upon causes out of our power, and part must be effected by vigour and perseverance. With regard to that which is styled in common language the work of chance, men will always find reasons for confidence or distrust, according to their different tempers or inclinations ; and he that has been long accustomed to please himself with possibilities of fortuitous happiness, will not easily or willingly be reclaimed from his mistake. But the effects of human industry and skill are more easily subjected to calculation : whatever can be completed in a year, is divisible into parts, of which each may be performed in the compass of a day[1] ; he, therefore, that has passed the day without attention to the task assigned him, may be certain that the lapse of life has brought him no nearer to his object ; for whatever idleness may

---

[1] Johnson recorded in his *Diary* on Advent-Sunday, 1774 :— " I began to read the Greek Testament regularly at 160 verses every Sunday." On this Boswell says :—" It is remarkable that he was very fond of the precision which calculation produces. Thus we find in one of his manuscript diaries, ' 12 pages in 4to. Gr. Test., and 30 pages in Beza's folio, comprise the whole in 40 days.' "—Boswell's *Johnson*, ii. 288.

expect from time, its produce will be only in proportion to the diligence with which it has been used. He that floats lazily down the stream, in pursuit of something borne along by the same current, will find himself indeed moved forward; but unless he lays his hand to the oar, and increases his speed by his own labour, must be always at the same distance from that which he is following.

There have happened in every age some contingencies of unexpected and undeserved success, by which those who are determined to believe whatever favours their inclinations, have been encouraged to delight themselves with future advantages; they support confidence by considerations, of which the only proper use is to chase away despair: it is equally absurd to sit down in idleness because some have been enriched without labour, as to leap a precipice because some have fallen and escaped with life, or to put to sea in a storm because some have been driven from a wreck upon the coast to which they were bound.

We are all ready to confess, that belief ought to be proportioned to evidence or probability: let any man, therefore, compare the number of those who have been thus favoured by fortune, and of those who have failed of their expectations, and he will easily determine, with what justness he has registered himself in the lucky catalogue.

But there is no need on these occasions for deep inquiries or laborious calculations; there is a far easier method of distinguishing the hopes of folly

II   H

from those of reason, of finding the difference between prospects that exist before the eyes, and those that are only painted on a fond imagination. Tom Drowsy had accustomed himself to compute the profit of a darling project, till he had no longer any doubt of its success; it was at last matured by close consideration, all the measures were accurately adjusted, and he wanted only five hundred pounds to become master of a fortune that might be envied by a director of a trading company. Tom was generous and grateful, and was resolved to recompense this small assistance with an ample fortune : he, therefore, deliberated for a time, to whom amongst his friends he should declare his necessities ; not that he suspected a refusal, but because he could not suddenly determine which of them would make the best use of riches, and was, therefore, most worthy of his favour. At last his choice was settled ; and knowing that in order to borrow he must shew the probability of re-payment, he prepared for a minute and copious explanation of his project. But here the golden dream was at an end : he soon discovered the impossibility of imposing upon others the notions by which he had so long imposed upon himself ; which way soever he turned his thoughts, impossibility and absurdity arose in opposition on every side ; even credulity and prejudice were at last forced to give way, and he grew ashamed of crediting himself what shame would not suffer him to communicate to another.

To this test let every man bring his imaginations, before they have been too long predominant in his mind. Whatever is true will bear to be related, whatever is rational will endure to be explained ; but when we delight to brood in secret over future happiness, and silently to employ our meditations upon schemes of which we are conscious that the bare mention would expose us to derision and contempt ; we should then remember, that we are cheating ourselves by voluntary delusions ; and giving up to the unreal mockeries of fancy, those hours in which solid advantages might be attained by sober thought and rational assiduity.

There is, indeed, so little certainty in human affairs, that the most cautious and severe examiner may be allowed to indulge some hopes which he cannot prove to be much favoured by probability ; since after his utmost endeavours to ascertain events, he must often leave the issue in the hands of chance. And so scanty is our present allowance of happiness, that in many situations life could scarcely be supported, if hope were not allowed to relieve the present hour by pleasures borrowed from futurity : and re-animate the languor of dejection to new efforts, by pointing to distant regions of felicity, which yet no resolution or perseverance shall ever reach.

But these, like all other cordials, though they may invigorate in a small quantity, intoxicate in a greater ; these pleasures, like the rest, are lawful only in certain circumstances, and to certain degrees ; they may be useful in a due subserviency to nobler purposes, but become dangerous and destructive when once they gain the ascendant in the heart : to soothe the mind to tranquillity by hope, even when that hope is likely to deceive us, may be sometimes useful ; but to lull our faculties in a lethargy, is poor and despicable.

Vices and errors are differently modified, according to the state of the minds to which they are incident ; to indulge hope beyond the warrant of reason, is the failure alike of mean and elevated understandings ; but its foundation and its effects are totally different : the man of high courage and great abilities is apt to place too much confidence in himself, and to expect from a vigorous exertion of his powers more than spirit or diligence can attain : between him and his wish he sees obstacles indeed, but he expects to overleap or break them ; his mistaken ardour hurries him forward ; and though perhaps he misses his end, he nevertheless obtains some collateral good, and performs something useful to mankind and honourable to himself.

The drone of timidity presumes likewise to hope, but without ground and without consequence; the bliss with which he solaces his hours, he always expects from others, though very often he knows not from whom : he folds his arms about him, and sits in expectation of some revolution in the state that shall raise him to greatness, or some golden shower that shall load him with wealth ; he dozes away the day in musing upon the morrow ; and at the end of life is roused from his dream only to discover that the time of action is past, and that he can now shew his wisdom only by repentance.

No. 99. TUESDAY, OCTOBER 16, 1753.

----· *Magnis tamen excidit ausis.*—Ovid.[1]

But in the glorious enterprise he died.—Addison.[2]

IT has always been the practice of mankind, to judge of actions by the event. The same attempts, conducted in the same manner, but terminated by different success, produce different judgments : they who attain their wishes, never want celebrators of their wisdom and their virtue ; and they that miscarry, are quickly discovered to have been defective not only in mental but in moral qualities. The world will never be long without some good reason to hate the unhappy : their real faults are immediately detected ; and if those are not sufficient to sink them into infamy, an additional weight of calumny will be superadded ; he that fails in his endeavours after wealth or power, will not long retain either honesty or courage.

This species of injustice has so long prevailed in universal practice, that it seems likewise to have infected speculation : so few minds are able to separate the ideas of greatness and prosperity, that even Sir William Temple has determined,

1 *Metamorphoses*, ii. 328.
2 Addison's *Works*, ed. 1862 i. 96.

"that he who can deserve the name of a hero,
"must not only be virtuous but fortunate."[1]

By this unreasonable distribution of praise and
blame, none have suffered oftener than projectors,
whose rapidity of imagination and vastness of
design raise such envy in their fellow-mortals,
that every eye watches for their fall, and every
heart exults at their distresses : yet even a projector may gain favour by success ; and the tongue
that was prepared to hiss, then endeavours to excel
others in loudness of applause.

When Coriolanus, in Shakespeare, deserted to
Aufidius, the Volscian servants at first insulted
him, even while he stood under the protection of
the household gods ; but when they saw that the
project took effect, and the stranger was seated at
the head of the table, one of them very judiciously
observes, "that he always thought there was more
"in him than he could think."[2]

Machiavel has justly animadverted on the
different notice taken by all succeeding times of
the two great projectors Catiline and Cæsar.
Both formed the same project, and intended to

[1] Johnson twice more quoted Temple's saying, once as
reported by Boswell in the *Life* (ii. 234), and once in writing
to Mrs. Thrale (*Piozzi Letters*, ii. 93). He refers, I believe,
to Temple's Essay *Of Heroick Virtue*, where that writer says
that "the excellency of genius" must not only "be cultivated
by education and instruction," but also "must be assisted by
fortune to preserve it to maturity ; because the noblest spirit
or genius in the world, if it falls, though never so bravely, in
its first enterprises, cannot deserve enough of mankind to
pretend to so great a reward as the esteem of heroic virtue."
[2] "But I thought there was more in him than I could
think."—*Coriolanus*, Act iv., sc. 5, l. 166.

raise themselves to power, by subverting the commonwealth ; they pursued their design, perhaps, with equal abilities, and with equal virtue ; but Catiline perished in the field, and Cæsar returned from Pharsalia with unlimited authority : and from that time, every monarch of the earth has thought himself honoured by a comparison with Cæsar ; and Catiline has been never mentioned, but that his name might be applied to traitors and incendiaries.

In an age more remote, Xerxes projected the conquest of Greece, and brought down the power of Asia against it : but after the world had been filled with expectation and terror, his army was beaten, his fleet was destroyed, and Xerxes has never been mentioned without contempt.

A few years afterwards, Greece likewise had her turn of giving birth to a projector ; who invading Asia with a small army, went forward in search of adventures, and by his escape from one danger, gained only more rashness to rush into another : he stormed city after city, over-ran kingdom after kingdom, fought battles only for barren victory, and invaded nations only that he might make his way through them to new invasions : but having been fortunate in the execution of his projects, he died with the name of Alexander the Great.

These are, indeed, events of ancient times ; but human nature is always the same, and every age will afford us instances of public censures influenced by events. The great business of the middle centuries, was the holy war; which undoubtedly was a noble project, and was for a long time prosecuted with a spirit equal to that with which it had been contrived : but the ardour of the European heroes only hurried them to destruction ; for a long time they could not gain the territories for which they fought, and, when at last gained, they could not keep them : their expeditions, therefore, have been the scoff of idleness and ignorance, their understanding and their virtue have been equally vilified, their conduct has been ridiculed, and their cause has been defamed.

When Columbus had engaged king Ferdinand in the discovery of the other hemisphere, the sailors, with whom he embarked in the expedition, had so little confidence in their commander, that after having been long at sea looking for coasts, which they expected never to find, they raised a general mutiny, and demanded to return. He found means to sooth them into a permission to continue the same course three days longer, and on the evening of the third day descried land. Had the impatience of his crew denied him a few hours of the time requested, what had been his fate but to have come back with the infamy of a vain projector, who had betrayed the king's credulity to useless expences, and risked his life in seeking countries that had no existence ? how would those that had rejected his proposals, have triumphed in their acuteness ? and when would his name have been mentioned, but with the makers of potable gold[1] and malleable glass.

---

[1] " *Tertio* monemus ut homines nugari desinant, nec tam faciles sint ut credant, grande illud opus quale est naturæ cursum remorari et retrovertere, posse haustu aliquo matutino,

The last royal projectors with whom the world has been troubled, were Charles of Sweden and the Czar of Muscovy. Charles, if any judgment may be formed of his designs by his measures and his inquiries, had purposed first to dethrone the Czar, then to lead his army through pathless deserts into China, thence to make his way by the sword through the whole circuit of Asia, and by the conquest of Turkey to unite Sweden with his new dominions: but this mighty project was crushed at Pultowa[1]; and Charles has since been considered as a madman by those powers, who sent their ambassadors to solicit his friendship, and their generals "to learn under him the art " of war."

The Czar found employment sufficient in his own dominions, and amused himself in digging canals, and building cities ; murdering his subjects with insufferable fatigues, and transplanting nations from one corner of his dominions to another, without regretting the thousands that perished on the way : but he attained his end; he made his people formidable, and is numbered by fame among the demi-gods.

---

aut usu alicujus pretiosæ medicinæ, ad exitum perduci : non auro potabili, non margaritarum essentiis, et similibus nugis." —Bacon's *Works*, ed. 1803, vii. 227.

[1] " The march begins in military state,
And nations on his eye suspended wait ;
Stern famine guards the solitary coast,
And winter barricades the realms of frost ;
He comes. nor want nor cold his course delay ;—
Hide, blushing glory, hide Pultowa's day."
—*The Vanity of Human Wishes*, 1. 205.

I am far from intending to vindicate the sanguinary projects of heroes and conquerors, and would
wish rather to diminish the reputation of their
success, than the infamy of their miscarriages : for
I cannot conceive, why he that has burnt cities,
wasted nations, and filled the world with horror
and desolation, should be more kindly regarded
by mankind, than he that died in the rudiments
of wickedness ; why he that accomplished mischief
should be glorious, and he that only endeavoured
it should be criminal. I would wish Cæsar and
Catiline, Xerxes and Alexander, Charles and
Peter, huddled together in obscurity or detestation.

But there is another species of projectors,
to whom I would willingly conciliate mankind ;
whose ends are generally laudable, and whose
labours are innocent ; who are searching out new
powers of nature, or contriving new works of art ;
but who are yet persecuted with incessant obloquy,
and whom the universal contempt with which they
are treated, often debars from that success which
their industry would obtain, if it were permitted
to act without opposition.

They who find themselves inclined to censure
new undertakings, only because they are new,
should consider, that the folly of projection is very
seldom the folly of a fool ; it is commonly the
ebullition of a capacious mind, crowded with
variety of knowledge, and heated with intenseness
of thought ; it proceeds often from the consciousness of uncommon powers, from the confidence of
those, who having already done much, are easily

persuaded that they can do more. When Rowley had completed the orrery,[1] he attempted the perpetual motion ; when Boyle had exhausted the secrets of vulgar chemistry, he turned his thoughts to the work of transmutation.[2]

A projector generally unites those qualities which have the fairest claim to veneration, extent of knowledge, and greatness of design ; it was said of Catiline, " immoderata, incredibilia, nimis " alta semper cupiebat."[3] Projectors of all kinds agree in their intellects, though they differ in their morals ; they all fail by attempting things beyond their power, by despising vulgar attainments, and aspiring to performances, to which,

---

[1] According to an account quoted in the *Penny Cylcopædia*, ed. 1840, xvii. 38, it was not Rowley, but George Graham who, about the year 1700, invented the orrery. Rowley, it seems, was an instrument-maker who made the first for the Earl of Orrery.

[2] Boyle had "a process for 'multiplying gold' by combining a certain red earth with mercury." Before his death he communicated it to Locke and Newton. Newton having received some of this earth from Locke told him " that though he had no inclination to prosecute the process," yet as he [Locke] had "a mind to prosecute it," he would be glad to assist him.—Brewster's *Life of Newton*, ed. 1855, ii. 121. Boswell says that " as to alchemy, Johnson was not a positive unbeliever, but rather delighted in considering what progress had actually been made in the transmutation of metals, what near approaches there had been to the making of gold." —Boswell's *Johnson*, ii. 376. The writer of the article on Robert Boyle in Knight's *Cyclo. of Biog.* points out "that faith in alchemy now and the same in the middle of the seventeenth century are two things so different in kind that to laugh at both in one shows nothing but the ignorance of the laugher."

[3] Sallust : *Catilina*, ch. 5.

perhaps, nature has not proportioned the force of man : when they fail, therefore, they fail not by idleness or timidity, but by rash adventure and fruitless diligence.

That the attempts of such men will often miscarry, we may reasonably expect ; yet from such men, and such only, are we to hope for the cultivation of those parts of nature which lie yet waste, and the invention of those arts which are yet wanting to the felicity of life. If they are, therefore, universally discouraged, art and discovery can make no advances.[1] Whatever is attempted without previous certainty of success, may be considered as a project, and amongst narrow minds may, therefore, expose its author to censure and contempt ; and if the liberty of laughing be once indulged, every man will laugh at what he does not understand, every project will be considered as madness and every great or new design will be censured as a project. Men, unaccustomed to reason and researches, think every enterprise impracticable, which is extended beyond common effects, or comprises many intermediate operations. Many that presume to laugh at projectors, would consider a flight through the air in a winged chariot, and the movement of a mighty engine by the steam

---

[1] An old sea-faring man wrote to Swift that he had found out the longitude. The Dean replied "that he never knew but two projectors, one of whom ruined himself and his family, and the other hanged himself ; and desired him to desist lest one or other might happen to him."—Swift's *Works*, ed. 1803, xvii. 157.

of water, as equally the dreams of mechanic lunacy ; and would hear with equal negligence, of the union of the Thames and Severn by a canal,[1] and the scheme of Albuquerque, the viceroy of the Indies, who in the rage of hostility had contrived[2] to make Egypt a barren desert, by turning the Nile into the Red Sea.

Those who have attempted much, have seldom failed to perform more than those who never deviate from the common roads of action : many valuable preparations of chemistry are supposed to have risen from unsuccessful inquiries after the grand elixir[3] : it is, therefore, just to encourage those who endeavour to enlarge the power of art, since they often succeed beyond expectation ; and when they fail, may sometimes benefit the world even by their miscarriages.

[1] No canal in England had as yet been made. " Their origin dates from the year 1755, when an Act of Parliament was passed for constructing one from the Mersey to St. Helens."—*Penny Cyclo.*, first ed., vi. 219. The Thames and Severn Canal was finished in 1789.

[2] Johnson defines *to contrive* as *to plan out ; to excogitate.* The sense of *planning out successfully* seems to be more modern than the date of his *Dictionary.* It was under Albuquerque that the Portuguese founded their rule in the East Indies, Johnson in his translation of Lobo's *Voyage to Abyssinia*, p. 218, says that, according to Albuquerque's son, " nothing more was required to turn the Nile into a new channel than to dig through a little mountain that lies along it in the country of Prester John."

[3] Johnson defines *elixir* as *the liquor, or whatever it be, with which chemists hope to transmute metals to gold.*

No. 108. SATURDAY, NOVEMBER 17, 1753.

'Nobis quum simul occidit brevis lux,
Nox est perpetuo una dormienda.—CATULLUS.[1]
'When once the short-lived mortal dies,
A night eternal seals his eyes.—ADDISON.

IT may have been observed by every reader, that there are certain topics which never are exhausted. Of some images and sentiments the mind of man may be said to be enamoured; it meets them, however often they occur, with the same ardour which a lover feels at the sight of his mistress, and parts from them with the same regret when they can no longer be enjoyed.

Of this kind are many descriptions which the poets have transcribed from each other, and their successors will probably copy to the end of time; which will continue to engage, or, as the French term it, to flatter the imagination, as long as human nature shall remain the same.

When a poet mentions the spring, we know that the zephyrs are about to whisper, that the groves are to recover their verdure, the linnets to warble forth their notes of love, and the flocks and herds to frisk over vales painted with flowers: yet, who is there so insensible of the beauties of nature, so little delighted with the renovation of the world,

[1] Catullus, v. 5.

as not to feel his heart bound at the mention of
the spring?

When night overshadows a romantic scene, all
is stillness, silence, and quiet; the poets of the
grove cease their melody, the moon towers over
the world in gentle majesty, men forget their
labours and their cares, and every passion and
pursuit is for a while suspended. All this we
know already, yet we hear it repeated without
weariness; because such is generally the life of
man, that he is pleased to think on the time when
he shall pause from a sense of his condition.

When a poetical grove invites us to its covert,
we know that we shall find what we have already
seen, a limpid brook murmuring over pebbles, a
bank diversified with flowers, a green arch that
excludes the sun, and a natural grot shaded with
myrtles[1]; yet who can forbear to enter the pleasing
gloom, to enjoy coolness and privacy, and gratify
himself once more by scenes with which nature
has formed him to be delighted?

Many moral sentiments likewise are so adapted
to our state, that we find approbation whenever
they solicit it, and are seldom read without exciting a gentle emotion in the mind: such is the
comparison of the life of man with the duration of
a flower, a thought which, perhaps, every nation

1 "While they ring round the same unvaried chimes
   With sure returns of still expected rhymes;
   Where'er you find 'the cooling western breeze,'
   In the next line it 'whispers through the trees;'
   If crystal streams 'with pleasing murmurs creep,'
   The reader's threaten'd (not in vain) with sleep."
   —Pope, *Essay on Criticism*, l. 348.

has heard warbled in its own language, from the inspired poets of the Hebrews to our own times : yet this comparison must always please, because every heart feels its justness, and every hour confirms it by example.

Such, likewise, is the precept that directs us to use the present hour, and refer nothing to a distant time, which we are uncertain whether we shall reach ; this every moralist may venture to inculcate, because it will always be approved, and because it is always forgotten.

This rule is, indeed, every day enforced, by arguments more powerful than the dissertations of moralists : we see men pleasing themselves with future happiness, fixing a certain hour for the completion of their wishes, and perishing some at a greater and some at a less distance from the happy time ; all complaining of their disappointments, and lamenting that they had suffered the years which Heaven allowed them, to pass without improvement, and deferred the principal purpose of their lives to the time when life itself was to forsake them.

It is not only uncertain, whether, through all the casualties and dangers which beset the life of man, we shall be able to reach the time appointed for happiness or wisdom ; but it is likely, that whatever now hinders us from doing that which our reason and conscience declare necessary to be done, will equally obstruct us in times to come. It is easy for the imagination, operating on things not yet existing, to please itself with scenes of unmingled felicity, or plan out courses of uniform

virtue : but good and evil are in real life inseparably united ; habits grow stronger by indulgence ;
and reason loses her dignity, in proportion as she
has oftener yielded to temptation : " he that can-
" not live well to-day," says Martial, " will be less
" qualified to live well to-morrow."[1]

Of the uncertainty of every human good, every
human being seems to be convinced ; yet this
uncertainty is voluntarily increased by unnecessary
delay, whether we respect external causes, or
consider the nature of our own minds. He that
now feels a desire to do right, and wishes to regulate his life according to his reason, is not sure
that, at any future time assignable, he shall be
able to rekindle the same ardour ; he that has
now an opportunity offered him of breaking loose
from vice and folly, cannot know, but that he shall
hereafter be more entangled, and struggle for
freedom without obtaining it.

We are so unwilling to believe any thing to our
own disadvantage, that we will always imagine
the perspicacity of our own judgment and the
strength of our resolution more likely to increase
than to grow less by time ; and, therefore, conclude, that the will to pursue laudable purposes,
will be always seconded by the power.

But however we may be deceived in calculating
the strength of our faculties, we cannot doubt the
uncertainty of that life in which they must be
employed : we see every day the unexpected
death of our friends and our enemies, we see new
graves hourly opened for men older and younger

" Qui non est hodie, cras minus aptus erit."

II   I

than ourselves, for the cautious and the careless, the dissolute and the temperate, for men who like us were providing to enjoy or improve hours now irreversibly cut off; we see all this, and yet, instead of living, let year glide after year in preparations to live.

Men are so frequently cut off in the midst of their projections,[1] that sudden death causes little emotion in them that behold it, unless it be impressed upon the attention by uncommon circumstances. I, like every other man, have out-lived multitudes, have seen ambition sink in its triumphs, and beauty perish in its bloom; but have been seldom so much affected as by the fate of Euryalus, whom I lately lost as I began to love him.

Euryalus had for some time flourished in a lucrative profession; but having suffered his imagination to be fired by an unextinguishable curiosity, he grew weary of the same dull round of life,[2] resolved to harass himself no longer with the drudgery of getting money, but to quit his

---

[1] Johnson gives in his *Dictionary* as one of the meanings of *projection; scheme, plan of action.*

[2] " Johnson repeated with great emotion Shenstone's lines:—
'Whoe'er has travell'd life's dull round,
 Where'er his stages may have been,
 May sigh to think he still has found
 The warmest welcome at an inn.' "
                    —Boswell's *Johnson*, ii. 452.
These verses, it should seem, were first published in Dodsley's *Collection of Poems*, vol. v., p. 51. As this did not appear till 1758, Shenstone borrowed the "life's dull round" from Johnson.

business and his profit, and enjoy for a few years
the pleasures of travel. His friends heard him
proclaim his resolution without suspecting that he
intended to pursue it; but he was constant to his
purpose, and with great expedition closed his
accounts and sold his moveables, passed a few
days in bidding farewell to his companions, and
with all the eagerness of romantic chivalry crossed
the sea in search of happiness. Whatever place
was renowned in ancient or modern history, whatever region art or nature had distinguished, he
determined to visit: full of design and hope he
landed on the continent; his friends expected
accounts from him of the new scenes that opened
in his progress, but were informed in a few days
that Euryalus was dead.

Such was the end of Euryalus. He is entered
that state, whence none ever shall return; and
can now only benefit his friends, by remaining
in their memories a permanent and efficacious
instance of the blindness of desire, and the uncertainty of all terrestrial good. But, perhaps, every
man has like me lost an Euryalus, has known a
friend die with happiness in his grasp; and yet
every man continues to think himself secure of
life, and defers to some future time of leisure what
he knows it will be fatal to have finally omitted.

It is, indeed, with this as with other frailties
inherent in our nature; the desire of deferring
to another time, what cannot be done without
endurance of some pain, or forbearance of some
pleasure, will, perhaps, never be totally overcome
or suppressed; there will always be something

that we shall wish to have finished, and be
nevertheless unwilling to begin : but against this
unwillingness it is our duty to struggle, and every
conquest over our passions will make way for an
easier conquest ; custom is equally forcible to[1]
bad and good ; nature will always be at variance
with reason, but will rebel more feebly as she is
oftener subdued.

The common neglect of the present hour is
more shameful and criminal, as no man is betrayed
to it by error, but admits it by negligence. Of
the instability of life, the weakest understanding
never thinks wrong, though the strongest often
omits to think justly : reason and experience are
always ready to inform us of our real state ; but
we refuse to listen to their suggestions, because
we feel our hearts unwilling to obey them : but,
surely, nothing is more unworthy of a reasonable
being, than to shut his eyes, when he sees the
road which he is commanded to travel, that he
may deviate with fewer reproaches from himself ;
nor could any motive to tenderness, except the
consciousness that we have all been guilty of the
same fault, dispose us to pity those who thus
consign themselves to voluntary ruin.

1 Johnson in his *Dictionary* quotes from Hooker :—" That
punishment which hath been sometimes *forcible to* bridle
sin."

No. 111. TUESDAY, NOVEMBER 27, 1753.

———*Quæ non fecimus ipsi,*
Vix ea nostra voco.—Ovid.[1]

The deeds of long-descended ancestors
Are but by grace of imputation ours.—Dryden.

THE evils inseparably annexed to the present condition of man, are so numerous and afflictive, that it has been, from age to age, the task of some to bewail, and of others to solace them ; and he, therefore, will be in danger of seeming a common enemy, who shall attempt to depreciate the few pleasures and felicities which nature has allowed us.

Yet I will confess, that I have sometimes employed my thoughts in examining the pretensions that are made to happiness, by the splendid and envied condition of life ; and have not thought the hour unprofitably spent, when I have detected the imposture of counterfeit advantages, and found disquiet lurking under false appearances of gaiety and greatness.

1 *Metamorphoses,* xiii. 140. The motto to the *Rambler* No. 46, is
    " Genus et proavos et quæ non fecimus ipsi,
    Vix ea nostra voco."
which Johnson translates,
        " Nought from my birth or ancestors I claim ;
        All is my own, my honour and my shame."

It is asserted by a tragic poet, that "est miser
" nemo nisi comparatus," "no man is miserable,
" but as he is compared with others happier
" than himself;" this position is not strictly and
philosophically true. He might have said with
rigorous propriety, that no man is happy but as
he is compared with the miserable; for such is
the state of this world, that we find in it absolute
misery, but happiness only comparative; we may
incur as much pain as we can possibly endure,
though we can never obtain as much happiness as
we might possibly enjoy.

Yet it is certain likewise, that many of our
miseries are merely comparative: we are often
made unhappy, not by the presence of any real
evil, but by the absence of some fictitious good;
of something which is not required by any real
want of nature, which has not in itself any power
of gratification, and which neither reason nor
fancy would have prompted us to wish, did we
not see it in the possession of others.

For a mind diseased with vain longings after
unattainable advantages, no medicine can be prescribed, but an impartial inquiry into the real
worth of that which is so ardently desired. It is
well known, how much the mind, as well as the
eye, is deceived by distance; and, perhaps, it will
be found, that of many imagined blessings it may
be doubted, whether he that wants or possesses
them has more reason to be satisfied with his lot.

The dignity of high birth and long extraction,
no man, to whom nature has denied it, can confer
upon himself; and, therefore, it deserves to be

considered, whether the want of that which can never be gained, may not easily be endured. It is true, that if we consider the triumph and delight with which most of those recount their ancestors who have ancestors to recount, and the artifices by which some who have risen to unexpected fortune endeavour to insert themselves into an honourable stem, we shall be inclined to fancy that wisdom or virtue may be had by inheritance, or that all the excellencies of a line of progenitors are accumulated on their descendant. Reason, indeed, will soon inform us, that our estimation of birth is arbitrary and capricious, and that dead ancestors can have no influence but upon imagination : let it then be examined, whether one dream may not operate in the place of another ; whether he that owes nothing to forefathers, may not receive equal pleasure from the consciousness of owing all to himself ; whether he may not, with little meditation, find it more honourable to found than to continue a family, and to gain dignity than transmit it ; whether if he receive no dignity from the virtues of his family, he does not likewise escape the danger of being disgraced by their crimes ; and whether he that brings a new name into the world, has not the convenience of playing the game of life without a stake, and opportunity of winning much though he has nothing to lose.[1]

---

[1] "I heard Dr. Johnson once say, 'I have great merit in being zealous for subordination and the honours of birth ; for I can hardly tell who was my grandfather.'"—Boswell's *Johnson*, ii. 261.

There is another opinion concerning happiness, which approaches much more nearly to universality; but which may, perhaps, with equal reason be disputed. The pretensions to ancestral honours many of the sons of earth easily see to be ill-grounded; but all agree to celebrate the advantage of hereditary riches, and to consider those as the minions of fortune, who are wealthy from their cradles, whose estate is "res non parta labore sed "relicta[1];" "the acquisition of another, not of "themselves;" and whom a father's industry has dispensed from a laborious attention to arts or commerce, and left at liberty to dispose of life as fancy shall direct them.

If every man were wise and virtuous, capable to discern the best use of time, and resolute to practise it; it might be granted, I think, without hesitation, that total liberty would be a blessing; and that it would be desirable to be left at large to the exercise of religious and social duties, without the interruption of importunate avocations.

But since felicity is relative, and that which is the means of happiness to one man may be to another the cause of misery, we are to consider what state is best adapted to human nature in its present degeneracy and frailty. And, surely, to far the greater number it is highly expedient, that they should by some settled scheme of duties be rescued from the tyranny of caprice, that they should be driven on by necessity through the paths of life with their attention confined to a

1 See *ante*, p. 78.

stated task, that they may be less at leisure to deviate into mischief at the call of folly.

When we observe the lives of those whom an ample inheritance has let loose to their own direction, what do we discover that can excite our envy? Their time seems not to pass with much applause from others, or satisfaction to themselves: many squander their exuberance of fortune in luxury and debauchery, and have no other use of money than to inflame their passions, and riot in a wide range of licentiousness; others, less criminal indeed, but, surely, not so much to be praised, lie down to sleep, and rise up to trifle, are employed every morning in finding expedients to rid themselves of the day, chase pleasure through all the places of public resort, fly from London to Bath, and from Bath to London, without any other reason for changing place, but that they go in quest of company as idle and as vagrant as themselves, always endeavouring to raise some new desire that they may have something to pursue, to rekindle some hope which they know will be disappointed, changing one amusement for another which a few months will make equally insipid, or sinking into languor and disease for want of something to actuate their bodies or exhilarate their minds.

Whoever has frequented those places, where idlers assemble to escape from solitude, knows that this is generally the state of the wealthy; and from this state it is no great hardship to be debarred. No man can be happy in total idleness: he that should be condemned to lie torpid

and motionless, " would fly for recreation," says
South, "to the mines and the galleys[1] ; " and
it is well, when nature or fortune find employment for those, who would not have known how
to procure it for themselves.

He, whose mind is engaged by the acquisition
or improvement of a fortune, not only escapes the
insipidity of indifference, and the tediousness of
inactivity, but gains enjoyments wholly unknown
to those, who live lazily on the toil of others ; for
life affords no higher pleasure than that of sur-
mounting difficulties, passing from one step of
success to another, forming new wishes, and seeing
them gratified.   He that labours in any great or
laudable undertaking, has his fatigues first supported by hope, and afterwards rewarded by joy ;
he is always moving to a certain end, and when
he has attained it, an end more distant invites
him to a new pursuit.

It does not, indeed, always happen, that diligence is fortunate ; the wisest schemes are broken
by unexpected accidents ; the most constant perseverance sometimes toils through life without a
recompence ; but labour, though unsuccessful, is
more eligible than idleness ; he that prosecutes a
lawful purpose by lawful means, acts always with
the approbation of his own reason ; he is animated

1 " The most voluptuous person, were he tied to follow
his hawks and his hounds, his dice and his courtships every
day, would find it the greatest torment that could befall him ;
he would fly to the mines and the galleys for his recreation,
and to the spade and the mattock for a diversion from the
misery of a continual uninterrupted pleasure."—Johnson's
Dictionary under *Galley.*

through the course of his endeavours by an expectation which, though not certain, he knows to be just; and is at last comforted in his disappointment, by the consciousness that he has not failed by his own fault.

That kind of life is most happy which affords us most opportunities of gaining our own esteem; and what can any man infer in his own favour from a condition to which, however prosperous, he contributed nothing, and which the vilest and weakest of the species would have obtained by the same right, had he happened to be the son of the same father?

To strive with difficulties, and to conquer them, is the highest human felicity; the next, is to strive, and deserve to conquer: but he whose life has passed without a contest, and who can boast neither success nor merit, can survey himself only as a useless filler of existence; and if he is content with his own character, must owe his satisfaction to insensibility.

Thus it appears that the satirist advised rightly, when he directed us to resign ourselves to the hands of Heaven, and to leave to superior powers the determination of our lot:

> *Permittes ipsis expendere Numinibus, quid*
> *Conveniat nobis, rebusque sit utile nostris :*
> *Carior est illis homo quam sibi.*[1]

> Intrust thy fortune to the powers above :
> Leave them to manage for thee, and to grant
> What their unerring wisdom sees thee want.
> In goodness as in greatness they excel :
> Ah! that we lov'd ourselves but half so well.—DRYDEN.

[1] Juvenal, *Satires* x. 347.

What state of life admits most happiness, is
uncertain ; but that uncertainty ought to repress
the petulance of comparison, and silence the
murmurs of discontent.

No. 120. SATURDAY, DECEMBER, 29, 1753.

————Ultima semper
Expectanda dies homini, dicique beatus
Ante obitum nemo supremaque funera debet.—OVID.[1]

But no frail man, however great or high,
Can be concluded blest before he die.—ADDISON.

THE numerous miseries of human life
have extorted in all ages an universal
complaint. The wisest of men terminated all his experiments in search
of happiness, by the mournful confession, that
"all is vanity[2];" and the ancient patriarchs
lamented, that "the days of their pilgrimage
were "few and evil."[3]

There is, indeed, no topic on which it is more
superfluous to accumulate authorities, nor any
assertion of which our own eyes will more easily
discover, or our sensations more frequently impress the truth, than, that misery is the lot of
man, that our present state is a state of danger
and infelicity.

When we take the most distant prospect of life,

-----

1 *Metamorphoses*, iii. 135.　　2 *Ecclesiastes* xii. 8.
8 *Genesis* xlvii. 9.

what does it present us but a chaos of unhappiness, a confused and tumultuous scene of labour and contest, disappointment and defeat? If we view past ages in the reflection of history, what do they offer to our meditation but crimes and calamities? One year is distinguished by a famine, another by an earthquake; kingdoms are made desolate, sometimes by wars, and sometimes by pestilence; the peace of the world is interrupted at one time by the caprices of a tyrant, at another by the rage of a conqueror. The memory is stored only with vicissitudes of evil; and the happiness, such as it is, of one part of mankind, is found to arise commonly from sanguinary success, from victories which confer upon them the power, not so much of improving life by any new enjoyment as of inflicting misery on others, and gratifying their own pride by comparative greatness.

But by him that examines life with a more close attention, the happiness of the world will be found still less than it appears. In some intervals of public prosperity, or to use terms more proper, in some intermissions of calamity, a general diffusion of happiness may seem to overspread a people; all is triumph and exultation, jollity and plenty; there are no public fears and dangers, and "no complainings in the streets."[1] But the condition of individuals is very little mended by this general calm: pain and malice and discontent still continue their havoc; the silent depredation goes incessantly forward; and the grave continues to be filled by the victims of sorrow.

[1] No complaining in our streets.—*Psalms* cxliv. 14.

He that enters a gay assembly, beholds the cheerfulness displayed in every countenance, and finds all sitting vacant and disengaged, with no other attention than to give or to receive pleasure ; would naturally imagine, that he had reached at last the metropolis of felicity, the place sacred to gladness of heart, from whence all fear and anxiety were irreversibly excluded. Such, indeed, we may often find to be the opinion of those, who from a lower station look up to the pomp and gaiety which they cannot reach : but who is there of those who frequent these luxurious assemblies, that will not confess his own uneasiness, or cannot recount the vexations and distresses that prey upon the lives of his gay companions ?[1]

The world, in its best state, is nothing more than a larger assembly of beings, combining to counterfeit happiness which they do not feel, employing every art and contrivance to embellish life, and to hide their real condition from the eyes of one another.

The species of happiness most obvious to the observation of others, is that which depends upon the goods of fortune ; yet even this is often fictitious. There is in the world more poverty

---

[1] Boswell and Johnson visited the Pantheon in Oxford Street on March 31, 1772. " 'I said there was not half a guinea's worth of pleasure in seeing this place.'—*Johnson.* 'But, sir, there is half a guinea's worth of inferiority to other people in not having seen it.'—*Boswell.* 'I doubt, sir, whether there are many happy people here.'—*Johnson.* 'Yes, sir, there are many happy people here. There are many people here who are watching hundreds, and who think hundreds are watching them.' "—Boswell's *Johnson,* ii. 169.

than is generally imagined; not only because many whose possessions are large have desires still larger, and many measure their wants by the gratifications which others enjoy : but great numbers are pressed by real necessities which it is their chief ambition to conceal, and are forced to purchase the appearance of competence and cheerfulness at the expence of many comforts and conveniences of life.

Many, however, are confessedly rich, and many more are sufficiently removed from all danger of real poverty : but it has been long ago remarked, that money cannot purchase quiet ; the highest of mankind can promise themselves no exemption from that discord or suspicion, by which the sweetness of domestic retirement is destroyed ; and must always be even more exposed, in the same degree as they are elevated above others, to the treachery of dependents, the calumny of defamers, and the violence of opponents.

Affliction is inseparable from our present state ; it adheres to all the inhabitants of this world, in different proportions indeed, but with an allotment which seems very little regulated by our own conduct. It has been the boast of some swelling moralists,[1] that every man's fortune was in his own power, that prudence supplied the place of all other divinities, and that happiness is the un-failing consequence of virtue. But, surely the

[1] Of the Psalmist among others, who says :—"I have been young and now am old ; and yet saw I never the righteous forsaken, nor his seed begging their bread."—*Psalms* xxxvii. 25.

quiver of Omnipotence is stored with arrows, against which the shield of human virtue, however adamantine it has been boasted, is held up in vain : we do not always suffer by our crimes; we are not always protected by our innocence.

A good man is by no means exempt from the danger of suffering by the crimes of others ; even his goodness may raise him enemies of implacable malice and restless perseverance : the good man has never been warranted by Heaven from the treachery of friends, the disobedience of children, or the dishonesty of a wife ; he may see his cares made useless by profusion, his instructions defeated by perverseness, and his kindness rejected by ingratitude : he may languish under the infamy of false accusations, or perish reproachfully by an unjust sentence.

A good man is subject, like other mortals, to all the influences of natural evil ; his harvest is not spared by the tempest, nor his cattle by the murrain ; his house flames like others in a conflagration ; nor have his ships any peculiar power of resisting hurricanes : his mind, however elevated, inhabits a body subject to innumerable casualties, of which he must always share the dangers and the pains ; he bears about him the seeds of disease, and may linger away a great part of his life under the tortures of the gout or stone ; at one time groaning with insufferable anguish, at another dissolved in listlessness and languor.

From this general and indiscriminate distribution of misery, the moralists have always derived one of their strongest moral arguments for a future state : for since the common events of the present life happen alike to the good and bad, it follows from the justice of the Supreme Being, that there must be another state of existence, in which a just retribution shall be made, and every man shall be happy and miserable according to his works.

The miseries of life may, perhaps, afford some proof of a future state, compared as well with the mercy as the justice of God. It is scarcely to be imagined, that Infinite Benevolence would create a being capable of enjoying so much more than is here to be enjoyed, and qualified by nature to pro-long pain by remembrance, and anticipate it by terror, if he was not designed for something nobler and better than a state, in which many of his faculties can serve only for his torment ; in which he is to be importuned by desires that never can be satisfied, to feel many evils which he had no power to avoid, and to fear many which he shall never feel : there will surely come a time when every capacity of happiness shall be filled, and none shall be wretched but by his own fault.[1]

In the mean time, it is by affliction chiefly that the heart of man is purified, and that the thoughts are fixed upon a better state. Prosperity, allayed and imperfect as it is, has power to intoxicate the imagination, to fix the mind upon the present scene, to produce confidence and elation, and to

---

[1] " All that virtue can afford is quietness of conscience, a steady prospect of a happier state ; this may enable us to endure calamity with patience, but remember that patience must suppose pain."—*Rasselas*, ch. 27.

II   K

make him who enjoys affluence and honours forget the hand by which they were bestowed. It is
seldom that we are otherwise, than by affliction,
awakened to a sense of our own imbecility, or
taught to know how little all our acquisitions can
conduce to safety or to quiet : and how justly we
may ascribe to the superintendence of a higher
Power, those blessings which in the wantonness of
success we considered as the attainments of our
policy or courage.

Nothing confers so much ability to resist the
temptations that perpetually surround us, as an
habitual consideration of the shortness of life, and
the uncertainty of those pleasures that solicit our
pursuit ; and this consideration can be inculcated
only by affliction. "O Death ! how bitter is the
remembrance of thee, to a man that lives at ease
in his possessions!" If our present state were
one continued succession of delights, or one uniform flow of calmness and tranquillity, we should
never willingly think upon its end ; death would
then surely surprise us as "a thief in the night ;"[1]
and our task of duty would remain unfinished,
till "the night came when no man can work."[2]

While affliction thus prepares us for felicity, we

[1] 1 *Thessalonians* v. 2.

[2] *St. John* ix. 4. On the dial-plate of Johnson's watch
was inscribed the first part of this verse in the Greek characters.
" He afterwards laid aside this dial-plate ; and when I asked
him the reason, he said, 'It might do very well upon a clock
which a man keeps in his closet ; but to have it upon his
watch which he carries about with him, and which is often
looked at by others, might be censured as ostentatious.' "—
Boswell's *Johnson*, ii. 57.

may console ourselves under its pressures, by remembering, that they are no particular marks of divine displeasure ; since all the distresses of per-secution have been suffered by those, " of whom the world was not worthy ;"[1] and the Redeemer of Mankind himself was " a man of sorrows and acquainted with grief."[2]

No. 131. TUESDAY, FEBRUARY 5, 1754.

——— *Misce*
Ergo aliquid nostris de moribus.—JUVENAL.[3]
And mingle something of our times to please.
—DRYDEN, jun.[4]

ONTENELLE, in his panegyric on Sir Isaac Newton, closes a long enumera-tion of that great philosopher's virtues and attainments, with an observation, that " he was not distinguished from other men by any singularity either natural or affected." [5]

It is an eminent instance of Newton's superiority to the rest of mankind, that he was able to sepa-rate knowledge from those weaknesses by which knowledge is generally disgraced ; that he was

· **1** *Hebrews* xi. 38.   **2** *Isaiah* liii. 3.   **8** *Satires* xiv. 322.

4 Dryden's sons " in 1693 appeared among the translators of Juvenal."—Johnson's *Works*, vii. 290.

5 " Il était simple, affable, toujours de niveau avec tout le monde. Les génies du premier ordre ne méprisent point cc qui est au-dessous d'eux, tandis que les autres méprisent même ce qui est au-dessus. Il ne se croyait dispensé, ni par son mérite, ni par sa réputation, d'aucun des devoirs du

able to excel in science and wisdom, without purchasing them by the neglect of little things, and that he stood alone merely because he had left the rest of mankind behind him, not because he deviated from the beaten track.

Whoever, after the example of Plutarch, should compare the lives of illustrious men, might set this part of Newton's character to view with great advantage, by opposing it to that of Bacon, perhaps the only man of later ages, who has any pretensions to dispute with him the palm of genius or science.

Bacon, after he had added to a long and careful contemplation of almost every other object of knowledge a curious inspection into common life, and after having surveyed nature as a philosopher, had examined " men's business and bosoms "[1] as a statesman ; yet failed so much in the conduct

commerce ordinaire de la vie ; nulle singularité, ni naturelle ni affectée ; il savait n'être, dès qu'il le fallait, qu'un homme du commun." *Œuvres de Fontenelle,* ed. 1818, i. 402. "There is in human nature (said Johnson) a general inclination to make people stare ; and every wise man has himself to cure of it, and does cure himself."—Boswell"s *Johnson,* ii. 74. Writing of Swift, he says :—"Whatever he did, he seemed willing to do in a manner peculiar to himself, without sufficiently considering that singularity, as it implies a contempt of the general practice, is a kind of defiance which justly provokes the hostility of ridicule."—Johnson's *Works,* viii. 223.

[1] "I do now publish my *Essays,* which of all my other works have been most current : for that, as it seems, they come home to men's business and bosoms."—Bacon's *Essays,* Dedication to the edition of 1625. Johnson had quoted this passage earlier in the *Rambler,* No. 106. "He told me," writes Boswell, "that Bacon was a favourite author with him, but he had

of domestic affairs, that, in the most lucrative post to which a great and wealthy kingdom could advance him, he felt all the miseries of distressful poverty, and committed all the crimes to which poverty incites. Such were at once his negligence and rapacity, that as it is said, he would gain by unworthy practices that money, which, when so acquired, his servants might steal from one end of the table, while he sat studious and abstracted at the other.

As scarcely any man has reached the excellence, very few have sunk to the weakness of Bacon; but almost all the studious tribe, as they obtain any participation of his knowledge, feel likewise some contagion of his defects; and obstruct the veneration which learning would procure, by follies greater or less, to which only learning could betray them.

It has been formerly remarked by The Guardian, that the world punishes with too great severity the error of those, who imagine that the ignorance of little things may be compensated by the knowledge of great; for so it is, that as more can detect petty failings than can distinguish or esteem great qualifications, and as mankind is in general

---

never read his works till he was compiling the *English Dictionary*, in which, he said, I might see Bacon very often quoted."—Boswell's *Johnson*, iii. 194. According to Sir Joshua Reynolds, " Mr. Burke, speaking of Bacon's *Essays*, said he thought them the best of his works. Dr. Johnson was of opinion that their excellence and their value consisted in being the observations of a strong mind operating upon life, and in consequence you find there what you seldom find in other books."—Northcote's *Life of Reynolds*, ii. 281.

more easily disposed to censure than to admiration, contempt is often incurred by slight mistakes
which real virtue or usefulness cannot counter-
balance.[1]

Yet such mistakes and inadvertencies, it is not
easy for a man deeply immersed in study to avoid ;
no man can become qualified for the common
intercourses of life, by private meditation ; the
manners of the world are not a regular system,
planned by philosophers upon settled principles,
in which every cause has a congruous effect, and
one part has a just reference to another. Of the
fashions prevalent in every country, a few have
arisen, perhaps, from particular temperatures of
the climate ; a few more from the constitution of
the government ; but the greater part have grown
up by chance ; been started by caprice, been contrived by affectation, or borrowed without any just
motives of choice from other countries.

Of all these, the savage that hunts his prey
upon the mountains, and the sage that speculates
in his closet, must necessarily live in equal ignorance ; yet by the observation of these trifles it
is, that the ranks of mankind are kept in order,
that the address of one to another is regulated,
and the general business of the world carried on
with facility and method.

1 " The indiscretion of believing that great qualities make
up for the want of things less considerable is punished too
severely in those who are guilty of it. Every day's experience
shows us, among variety of people with whom we are not
acquainted, that we take impressions too favourable and too
disadvantageous of men at first sight from their habit."—
Guardian, No. 10, by Steele.

These things, therefore, though small in themselves, become great by their frequency; and he
very much mistakes his own interest, who, to the
unavoidable unskilfulness of abstraction and retirement, adds a voluntary neglect of common forms,
and increases the disadvantages of a studious
course of life by an arrogant contempt of those
practices, by which others endeavour to gain
favour and multiply friendships.[1]

A real and interior disdain of fashion and cere-
mony, is, indeed, not very often to be found:
much the greater part of those who pretend to
laugh at foppery and formality, secretly wish to
have possessed those qualifications which they
pretend to despise : and because they find it
difficult to wash away the tincture which they
have so deeply imbibed, endeavour to harden
themselves in a sullen approbation of their own
colour. Neutrality is a state, into which the
busy passions of man cannot easily subside ; and
he who is in danger of the pangs of envy, is
generally forced to recreate his imagination with
an effort of comfort.

[1] "Mr. Johnson," writes Mrs. Piozzi, "was indeed unjustly supposed to be a lover of singularity. Few people had
a more settled reverence for the world than he, or was less
captivated by new modes of behaviour introduced, or innova-
tions on the long-received customs of common life."—Piozzi's
Anecdotes, p. 108. Addison in the *Tatler*, No. 103, had
attacked singularity. "However slightly," he writes, "men
may regard these particularities and little follies in dress and
behaviour, they lead to greater evils. The bearing to be
laughed at for such singularities teaches us insensibly an
impertinent fortitude, and enables us to bear public censure
for things which more substantially deserve it."

Some, however, may be found, who, supported by the consciousness of great abilities, and elevated by a long course of reputation and applause, voluntarily consign themselves to singularity, affect to cross the roads of life because they know that they shall not be justled, and indulge a boundless gratification of will because they perceive that they shall be quietly obeyed. Men of this kind are generally known by the name of Humourists, an appellation by which he that has obtained it, and can be contented to keep it, is set free at once from the shackles of fashion : and can go in or out, sit or stand, be talkative or silent, gloomy or merry, advance absurdities or oppose demonstration, without any other reprehension from mankind, than that it is his way, that he is an odd fellow, and must be let alone.

This seems to many an easy passport through the various factions of mankind ; and those on whom it is bestowed, appear too frequently to consider the patience with which their caprices are suffered as an undoubted evidence of their own importance, of a genius to which submission is universally paid, and whose irregularities are only considered as consequences of its vigour. These peculiarities, however, are always found to spot a character, though they may not totally obscure it ; and he who expects from mankind, that they should give up established customs in compliance with his single will, and exacts that deference which he does not pay, may be endured, but can never be approved.

Singularity is, I think, in its own nature

universally and invariably displeasing. In whatever respect a man differs from others, he must
be considered by them as either worse or better :
by being better, it is well known that a man
gains admiration oftener than love, since all
approbation of his practice must necessarily
condemn him that gives it : and though a man
often pleases by inferiority, there are few who
desire to give such pleasure. Yet the truth is,
that singularity is almost always regarded as a
brand of slight reproach ; and where it is associated with acknowledged merit, serves as an
abatement or an allay of excellence, by which
weak eyes are reconciled to its lustre, and by
which, though kindness is not gained, at least
envy is averted.

But let no man be in haste to conclude his
own merit so great or conspicuous as to require
or justify singularity : it is as hazardous for a
moderate understanding to usurp the prerogatives
of genius, as for a common form to play over
the airs of uncontested beauty. The pride of
men will not patiently endure to see one, whose
understanding or attainments are but level with
their own, break the rules by which they have
consented to be bound, or forsake the direction
which they submissively follow. All violation of
established practice implies in its own nature a
rejection of the common opinion, a defiance of
common censure, and an appeal from general
laws to private judgment : he, therefore, who
differs from others without apparent advantage,
ought not to be angry if his arrogance is

punished with ridicule ; if those, whose example
he superciliously overlooks, point him out to derision, and hoot him back again into the common
road.

The pride of singularity is often exerted in
little things, where right and wrong are inde-
terminable, and where, therefore, vanity is without excuse.   But there are occasions on which it
is noble to dare to stand alone.   To be pious
among infidels, to be disinterested in a time
of general venality, to lead a life of virtue and
reason in the midst of sensualists, is a proof of
a mind intent on nobler things than the praise
or blame of men, of a soul fixed in the contemplation of the highest good, and superior to
the tyranny of custom and example.

In moral and religious questions only, a wise
man will hold no consultations with fashion,
because these duties are constant and immutable,
and depend not on the notions of men, but the
commands of Heaven : yet even of these, the
external mode is to be in some measure regulated by the prevailing taste of the age in which
we live ; for he is certainly no friend of virtue,
who neglects to give it any lawful attraction, or
suffers it to deceive the eye or alienate the
affections for want of innocent compliance with
fashionable decorations.[1]

1 Johnson did not avoid singularity when, in Scotland, he
refused to attend the services of the Established Church.   " I
will hear Dr. Robertson (said he) if he will get up into a tree
and preach ; but I will not give a sanction by my presence to
a Presbyterian assembly."—Boswell's *Johnson,* v. 121.

It is yet remembered of the learned and pious Nelson, that he was remarkably elegant in his manners, and splendid in his dress.[1] He knew, that the eminence of his character drew many eyes upon him ; and he was careful not to drive the young or the gay away from religion, by representing it as an enemy to any distinction or enjoyment in which human nature may innocently delight.

In this censure of singularity, I have, therefore, no intention to subject reason or conscience to custom or example. To comply with the notions and practices of mankind, is in some degree the duty of a social being ; because by compliance only he can please, and by pleasing only he can become useful : but as the end is not to be lost for the sake of the means, we are not to give up virtue to complaisance ; for the end of complaisance is only to gain the kindness of our fellow-beings, whose kindness is desirable only as instrumental to happiness, and happiness must be always lost by departure from virtue.

[1] Boswell says that "he understands that the excellent Mr. Nelson's *Festivals and Fasts* has the greatest sale of any book ever printed in England, except the Bible."—Boswell's *Johnson*, ii. 458. According to Mr. Seward, " Dr. Johnson always supposed that Mr. Richardson had Mr. Nelson in his thoughts when he delineated the character of Sir Charles Grandison."—Seward's *Anecdotes*, ii. 223.

THE IDLER.

THE IDLER

THE IDLER.

Duplici tibi dote....ty quod verum....
Et quod pradent...iam consilio snout.—Phaedrus [1]
Χάρις......

No. 4. SATURDAY, MAY 6, 1758.

Έλεστ γάρ φιλάνθρωπα.—Hom.[2]

CHARITY, or tenderness for the poor,
which is now justly considered, by a
great part of mankind, as inseparable
from piety, and in which almost all
the goodness of the present age consists, is, I

---

[1] Phaedrus, lib. i., prologue, l. 3.

[2] *Iliad*, vi. 14.

"A friend to human race."—Pope.

* J. Cradock says that Dr. Percy the night of his arrival in
London from Northumberland remembered that he had to
preach a charity-sermon next day. "Being much fatigued,
suddenly recollecting that Johnson's fourth *Idler* was exactly
to his purpose, he had freely engrafted the greatest part of it.
His discourse was much admired; but being requested to
print it, he most strenuously opposed the honour intended
him, till he was assured by the Governors that it was necessary, as the annual contributions greatly depended on it. He
earnestly requested that I would call upon Dr. Johnson,

THE IDLER.

Duplex libelli dos est, quod risum movet,
Et quod prudenti vitam consilio monet.—PHÆDRUS [1]
Χάρις μικροῖσι.

No. 4. SATURDAY, MAY 6, 1758.*

Πάντας γὰρ φιλέεσκε.—HOM.[2]

CHARITY, or tenderness for the poor, which is now justly considered, by a great part of mankind, as inseparable from piety, and in which almost all the goodness of the present age consists, is, I

[1] Phædrus, bk. i., prologue, l. 3.
[2] *Iliad*, vi. 15.
"A friend to human race."—POPE.

* J. Cradock says that Dr. Percy the night of his arrival in London from Northumberland remembered that he had to preach a charity-sermon next day. "Being much fatigued, suddenly recollecting that Johnson's fourth *Idler* was exactly to his purpose, he had freely engrafted the greatest part of it. His discourse was much admired ; but being requested to print it, he most strenuously opposed the honour intended him, till he was assured by the Governors that it was necessary, as the annual contributions greatly depended on it. He earnestly requested that I would call upon Dr. Johnson,

think, known only to those who enjoy, either immediately or by transmission, the light of revelation.

Those ancient nations who have given us the wisest models of government, and the brightest examples of patriotism, whose institutions have been transcribed by all succeeding legislatures, and whose history is studied by every candidate for political or military reputation, have yet left behind them no mention of alms-houses or hospitals, of places where age might repose, or sickness be relieved.

The Roman emperors, indeed, gave large donatives to the citizens and soldiers, but these distributions were always reckoned rather popular than virtuous : nothing more was intended than an ostentation of liberality, nor was any recompence expected, but suffrages and acclamations.

Their beneficence was merely occasional; he that ceased to need the favour of the people, ceased likewise to court it ; and, therefore, no man thought it either necessary or wise to make any standing provision for the needy, to look forwards

---

and state particulars. I assented ; and endeavoured to introduce the subject with all due solemnity ; but Johnson was highly diverted, and laughing, said:—'Pray, Sir, give my kind respects to Dr. Percy, and tell him I desire he will do whatever he pleases in regard to my *Idler ;* it is entirely at his service.'"—Cradock's *Memoirs*, ed. 1828, i. 242. The sermon, I have no doubt, was the one preached before the Sons of the Clergy on May 11, 1769 ; published by J. and F. Rivington. It is in the Bodleian Library. Johnson's thoughts are borrowed, but not his words.

to the wants of posterity, or to secure successions of charity, for successions of distress.

Compassion is by some reasoners, on whom the name of philosophers has been too easily conferred, resolved into an affection merely selfish, an involuntary perception of pain at the involuntary sight of a being like ourselves languishing in misery. But this sensation, if ever it be felt at all from the brute instinct of uninstructed nature, will only produce effects desultory and transient; it will never settle into a principle of action, or extend relief to calamities unseen, in generations not yet in being.

The devotion of life or fortune to the succour of the poor, is a height of virtue, to which humanity has never risen by its own power. The charity of the *Mahometans* is a precept which their teacher evidently transplanted from the doctrines of Christianity; and the care with which some of the Oriental sects attend, as is said, to the necessities of the diseased and indigent, may be added to the other arguments, which prove *Zoroaster* to have borrowed his institutions from the law of *Moses.*

The present age, though not likely to shine hereafter among the most splendid periods of history, has yet given examples of charity, which may be very properly recommended to imitation.[1]

---

[1] Goldsmith had this passage in mind when, four years later, he wrote in his *Life of Nash* :—" If I were to name any reigning and fashionable virtue in the present age, I think it should be charity. The numberless benefactions privately given, the various public solicitations for charity,

The equal distribution of wealth, which long commerce has produced, does not enable any single hand to raise edifices of piety like fortified cities, to appropriate manors to religious uses, or deal out such large and lasting beneficence as was scattered over the land in ancient times, by those who possessed counties or provinces. But no sooner is a new species of misery brought to view, and a design of relieving it professed, than every hand is open to contribute something, every tongue is busied in solicitation, and every art of pleasure is employed for a time in the interest of virtue.

The most apparent and pressing miseries incident to man, have now their peculiar houses of reception and relief ;[1] and there are few among us raised however little above the danger of poverty, who may not justly claim, what is implored by the *Mahometans* in their most ardent benedictions, the prayers of the poor.

Among those actions which the mind can most securely review with unabated pleasure, is that of having contributed to an hospital for the sick. Of some kinds of charity the consequences are dubious ; some evils which beneficence has been

---

and the success they meet with, serve to prove that though we may fall short of our ancestors in other respects, yet in this instance we greatly excel them."—Goldsmith's *Works*, iv. 78.

[1] "There are some parishes in these cities [London and Westminster] in which all the children die in the hands of parish nurses. Out of 174 brought into one parish work-house in two years only eleven survived."—Hanway's *Journal of Eight Days' Journey*, ed. 1756, p. 235.

busy to remedy, are not certainly known to be
very grievous to the sufferer, or detrimental to the
community ; but no man can question whether
wounds and sickness are not really painful ;
whether it be not worthy of a good man's care to
restore those to ease and usefulness, from whose
labour infants and women expect their bread, and
who, by a casual hurt, or lingering disease, lie
pining in want and anguish, burthensome to
others, and weary of themselves.

Yet as the hospitals of the present time subsist
only by gifts bestowed at pleasure, without any
solid fund of support, there is danger lest the
blaze of charity, which now burns with so much
heat and splendor, should die away for want of
lasting fuel ; lest fashion should suddenly withdraw her smile, and inconstancy transfer the
public attention to something which may appear
more eligible, because it will be new.

Whatever is left in the hands of chance must
be subject to vicissitude ; and when any establishment is found to be useful, it ought to be the next
care to make it permanent.

But man is a transitory being, and his designs
must partake of the imperfections of their author.
To confer duration is not always in our power.
We must snatch the present moment, and employ
it well, without too much solicitude for the future,
and content ourselves with reflecting that our part
is performed. He that waits for an opportunity
to do much at once, may breathe out his life in
idle wishes, and regret, in the last hour, his useless intentions, and barren zeal.

Tne most active promoters of the present
schemes of charity, cannot be cleared from some
instances of misconduct, which may awaken contempt or censure, and hasten that neglect which
is likely to come too soon of itself. The open
competitions between different hospitals, and the
animosity with which their patrons oppose one
another, may prejudice weak minds against them
all. For it will not be easily believed, that any
man can, for good reasons, wish to exclude another
from doing good. The spirit of charity can only
be continued by a reconciliation of these ridiculous feuds ; and therefore, instead of contentions
who shall be the only benefactors to the needy,
let there be no other struggle than who shall be
the first.[1]

[1] Fielding, in his *Covent Garden Journal*, No. 44, had
six years earlier written in a very different strain. He says :
—" If a man hath lived any time in the world, he must have
observed such horrid and notorious abuses of all public
charities, that he must be convinced (with a very few exceptions) that he will do no manner of good by contributing to
them. Some, indeed, are so very wretchedly contrived in
their institution that they seem not to have had the public
utility in their view ; but to have been mere jobs *ab initio*.
Such are all hospitals whatever, where it is a matter of
favour to get a patient admitted, and where the forms of ad-
mission are so troublesome and tedious, that the properest
objects (those, I mean, who are most wretched and friendless)
may as well aspire at a place at Court as at a place in the
hospital."

No. 8. SATURDAY, JUNE 3, 1758.

To the IDLER.

SIR,

IN the time of public danger,[1] it is every man's duty to withdraw his thoughts in some measure from his private interest, and employ part of his time for the general welfare. National conduct ought to be the result of national wisdom, a plan formed by mature consideration and diligent selection out of all the schemes which may be offered, and all the information which can be procured.

In a battle every man should fight as if he was the single champion; in preparations for war, every man should think as if the last event depended on his counsel. None can tell what discoveries are within his reach, or how much he may contribute to the public safety.

Full of these considerations, I have carefully reviewed the process of the war, and find, what every other man has found, that we have hitherto added nothing to our military reputation : that at

---

[1] On June 1, an armament had sailed for St. Malo, on one of those ill-planned and ill-conducted expeditions in the beginning of Pitt's administration, which were speedily to be followed by a succession of victories and conquests. Johnson's mockery of the army in a time of war is worthy of remark. In the fifth number he had described how "the soldiers must obey the call of their duty, and go to that side of the kingdom which faces France."

one time we have been beaten by enemies whom we did not see ; and, at another, have avoided the sight of enemies lest we should be beaten.

Whether our troops are defective in discipline or in courage, is not very useful to inquire ; they evidently want something necessary to success ; and he that shall supply that want will deserve well of his country.

To learn of an enemy has always been accounted politic and honourable[1] ; and therefore I hope it will raise no prejudices against my project, to confess that I borrowed it from a Frenchman

When the Isle of Rhodes was, many centuries ago, in the hands of that military order now called the Knights of Malta, it was ravaged by a dragon, who inhabited a den under a rock, from which he issued forth when he was hungry or wanton, and without fear or mercy devoured men and beasts as they came in his way. Many councils were held, and many devices offered for his destruction ; but as his back was armed with impenetrable scales none would venture to attack him. At last Dudon, a French knight, undertook the deliverance of the island. From some place of security he took a view of the dragon, or, as a modern soldier would say, *reconnoitred*[2] him, and observed

---

[1] "Fas est et ab hoste doceri."—Ovid, *Metamorphoses,* iv. 428.

[2] Addison in *The Spectator,* No. 165, gives a letter which a young gentleman in the army had written to his father, " very modishly chequered with modern military eloquence. The father, upon the perusal of it, found it contained great news, but could not guess what it was. He immediately communicated it to the curate of the parish, who, upon the

that his belly was naked and vulnerable. He then returned home to take his *arrangements*,[1] and, by a very exact imitation of nature, made a dragon of pasteboard, in the belly of which he put beef and mutton, and accustomed two sturdy mastiffs to feed themselves by tearing their way to the concealed flesh. When his dogs were well praetised in this method of plunder, he marched out with them at his heels, and shewed them the dragon ; they rushed upon him in quest of their dinner. Dudon battered his skull, while they lacerated his belly, and neither his sting nor claws were able to defend him.

Something like this might be practised in our present state. Let a fortification be raised on Salisbury Plain, resembling Brest or Toulon, or Paris itself, with all the usual preparation for defence : let the inclosure be filled with beef and ale : let the soldiers, from some proper eminence, see shirts waving upon lines, and here and there a plump landlady hurrying about with pots in their hands. When they are sufficiently animated to advance, lead them in exact order, with

---

reading of it, being vexed to see anything he could not understand, fell into a kind of passion." The letter begins : —"*U*pon the junction of the *F*rench and Bavarian armies, they took post behind a great morass which they thought impracticable. Our general the next day sent a party of horse to reconnoitre them from a little hauteur." Addison remarks :—"I do not find in any of our chronicles that Edward the Third ever reconnoitred the enemy."

[1] In later editions this has been wrongly printed " make his *arrangements*." Johnson is giving a phrase altogether "innovated from the *F*rench "—*prendre ses arrangements.*

fife and drum, to that side whence the wind blows,
till they come within the scent of roast meat and
tobacco.   Contrive that they may approach the
place fasting about an hour after dinner-time,
assure them there is no danger, and command an
attack.

If nobody within either moves or speaks, it is
not unlikely that they may carry the place by
storm ; but if a panic should seize them it will be
proper to defer the enterprize to a more hungry
hour.   When they have entered let them fill their
bellies and return to the camp.

On the next day let the same place be shewn
them again, but with some additions of strength
or terror.   I cannot pretend to inform our generals
through what gradations of danger they should
train their men to fortitude.   They best know
what the soldiers and what themselves can bear.
It will be proper that the war should every day
vary its appearance.   Sometimes, as they mount
the rampart, a cook may throw fat upon the fire
to accustom them to a sudden blaze ; and sometimes, by the clatter of empty pots, they may be
inured to formidable noises.   But let it never be
forgotten that victory must repose with a full
belly.

In time it will be proper to bring our French
prisoners from the coast, and place them upon the
walls in martial order.   At their first appearance
their hands must be tied, but they may be allowed
to grin.   In a month they may guard the place
with their hands loosed, provided that on pain of
death they be forbidden to strike.

By this method our army will soon be brought to look an enemy in the face. But it has been lately observed, that fear is received by the ear as well as the eyes ; and the Indian war-cry is represented as too dreadful to be endured ; as a sound that will force the bravest veteran to drop his weapon, and desert his rank ; that will deafen his ear, and chill his breast ; that will neither suffer him to hear orders nor to feel shame, or retain any sensibility but the dread of death.

That the savage clamours of naked barbarians should thus terrify troops disciplined to war, and ranged in array with arms in their hands, is surely strange. But this is no time to reason. I am of opinion, that by a proper mixture of asses, bulls, turkeys, geese, and tragedians,[1] a noise might be procured equally horrid with the war-cry. When our men have been encouraged by frequent victories, nothing will remain but to qualify them for extreme danger by a sudden concert of terrific vociferation. When they have endured this last trial let them be led to action, as men who are no longer to be frightened ; as men who can bear at once the grimaces of the Gauls, and the bowl of the Americans.

[1] Boswell mentions among Johnson's "heterodox opinions, a contempt of tragic acting."—Boswell's *Johnson*, v. 38.

No. 11. SATURDAY, JUNE 24, 1758.

I T is commonly observed, that when two Englishmen meet, their first talk is of the weather; they are in haste to tell each other, what each must already know, that it is hot or cold, bright or cloudy, windy or calm.[1]

There are, among the numerous lovers of subtilties and paradoxes, some who derive the civil institutions of every country from its climate, who impute freedom and slavery to the temperature of the air, can fix the meridians of vice and virtue, and tell at what degree of latitude we are to expect courage or timidity, knowledge or ignorance.

From these dreams of idle speculation, a slight survey of life, and a little knowledge of history, is sufficient to awaken any inquirer, whose ambition of distinction has not overpowered his love of truth.   Forms of government are seldom the result of much deliberation ; they are framed by chance in popular assemblies, or in conquered countries by despotic authority.   Laws are often

1 " There was no information (says Dr. Burney) for which Johnson was less grateful than for that which concerned the weather. If anyone of his acquaintance told him it was hot or cold, wet or dry, windy or calm, he would stop them by saying, ' Poh ! Poh ! you are telling us that of which none but men in a mine or a dungeon can be ignorant.' "   A few months before his death he wrote to Burney :—" The weather, you know, has not been balmy ; I am now reduced to think, and am at last content to talk, of the weather. Pride must have a fall."—Boswell's *Johnson*, iv. 360.

occasional, often capricious, made always by a
few, and sometimes by a single voice. Nations
have changed their characters; slavery is now no
where more patiently endured, than in countries
once inhabited by the zealots of liberty.

But national customs can arise only from
general agreement; they are not imposed, but
chosen, and are continued only by the continuance
of their cause. An Englishman's notice of the
weather, is the natural consequence of changeable
skies and uncertain seasons. In many parts of the
world, wet weather and dry are regularly expected
at certain periods; but in our island every man
goes to sleep, unable to guess whether he shall
behold in the morning a bright or cloudy atmo-
sphere, whether his rest shall be lulled by a shower,
or broken by a tempest.[1] We therefore rejoice
mutually at good weather, as at an escape from
something that we feared; and mutually complain
of bad, as of the loss of something that we hoped.

Such is the reason of our practice; and who
shall treat it with contempt? Surely not the
attendant on a court, whose business is to watch
the looks of a being weak and foolish as himself,[2]

[1] In his translation in *The Rambler*, No. 117, of some lines
of Tibullus he makes both shower and tempest lull to rest:—
  " How sweet in sleep to pass the careless hours,
  Lulled by the beating winds and dashing showers."

[2] It was George II. who was reigning when Johnson
wrote this—a king against whom he roared with prodigious
violence" (Boswell's *Johnson*, ii. 342). Boswell, quoting
the passage in the text, says:—"In this number of his
Idler his spirits seem to run riot; for in the wantonness
of his disquisition he forgets for a moment even the reverence
for that which he held in high respect."—*Ib.*, i. 333.

and whose vanity is to recount the names of
men, who might drop into nothing, and leave no
vacuity ; nor the proprietor of funds, who stops
his acquaintance in the street to tell him of the
loss of half-a-crown ; nor the inquirer after news,
who fills his head with foreign events, and talks
of skirmishes and sieges, of which no consequence
will ever reach his hearers or himself. The
weather is a nobler and more interesting subject ;
it is the present state of the skies and of the earth,
on which plenty and famine are suspended, on
which millions depend for the necessaries of life.

The weather is frequently mentioned for
another reason, less honourable to my dear
countrymen. Our dispositions too frequently
change with the colour of the sky ; and when we find
ourselves cheerful and good-natured, we naturally
pay our acknowledgments to the powers of sunshine ; or, if we sink into dulness and peevishness,
look round the horizon for an excuse, and charge
our discontent upon an easterly wind or a cloudy day.

Surely nothing is more reproachful to a being
endowed with reason, than to resign its powers to
the influence of the air, and live in dependence on
the weather and the wind, for the only blessings
which nature has put into our power, tranquillity
and benevolence.[1] To look up to the sky for the

---

[1] Boswell, quoting this passage and the last paragraph but
one in this *Idler*, remarks :—"He treats with the utmost
contempt the opinion that our mental faculties depend in some
degree upon the weather ; an opinion which they who have
never experienced its truth are not to be envied, and of which
he himself could not but be sensible, as the effects of weather
upon him were very visible."—Boswell's *Johnson*, i. 332.

nutriment of our bodies, is the condition of nature ; to call upon the sun for peace and gaiety, to deprecate the clouds lest sorrow should overwhelm us, is the cowardice of idleness, and the idolatry of folly.

Yet even in this age of inquiry and knowledge, when superstition is driven away,[1] and omens and prodigies have lost their terrors, we find this folly countenanced by frequent examples.   Those that laugh at the portentous glare of a comet, and hear a crow with equal tranquillity from the right or left, will yet talk of times and situations proper for intellectual performances, will imagine the fancy exalted by vernal breezes, and the reason invigorated by a bright calm.

If men who have given up themselves to fanciful credulity would confine their conceits in their own minds, they might regulate their lives by the barometer, with inconvenience only to themselves ; but to fill the world with accounts of intellects subjects to ebb and flow, of one genius that awakened in the spring, and another that ripened in the autumn,[2] of one mind expanded in

---

[1] Johnson, many years later, " came away from the Hebrides willing to believe the second sight."—Boswell's *Johnson*, ii. 318.

[2] Johnson in his *Life of Milton* ridicules the statement that that poet's poetical force depended on the time of the year. " The dependance of the soul upon the seasons, those temporary and periodical ebbs and flows of intellect, may, I suppose, justly be derided as the fumes of vain imagination. ' Sapiens   dominabitur   astris.' " — Johnson's *Works*, vii. 102.   Nevertheless, a few years earlier he had recorded in his *Diary* :—" Between Easter and Whitsuntide, having always considered that time as propitious to study, I attempted to learn the Low-Dutch language." — Boswell's *Johnson*, i. 332, *n.* 2.

the summer, and of another concentrated in the winter, is no less dangerous than to tell children of bugbears and goblins. Fear will find every house haunted ; and idleness will wait for ever for the moment of illumination.

This distinction of seasons is produced only by imagination operating on luxury. To temperance every day is bright, and every hour is propitious to diligence. He that shall resolutely excite his faculties, or exert his virtues, will soon make himself superior to the seasons, and may set at defiance the morning mist, and the evening damp, the blasts of the east, and the clouds of the south.

It was the boast of the *Stoic* philosophy, to make man unshaken by calamity, and unelated by success, incorruptible by pleasure, and invulnerable by pain ; these are heights of wisdom which none ever attained, and to which few can aspire ; but there are lower degrees of constancy necessary to common virtue ; and every man, however he may distrust himself in the extremes of good or evil ; might at least struggle against the tyranny of the climate, and refuse to enslave his virtue or his reason to the most variable of all variations, the changes of the weather.

No. 16. SATURDAY, JULY 29, 1758.

I PAID a visit yesterday to my old friend Ned Drugget, at his country lodgings. Ned began trade with a very small fortune ; he took a small house in an obscure street, and for some years dealt only in remnants. Knowing that *light gains make a heavy purse*, he was content with moderate profit ; having observed or heard the effects of civility, he bowed down to the counter edge at the entrance and departure of every customer, listened without impatience to the objections of the ignorant, and refused without resentment the offers of the penurions. His only recreation was to stand at his own door and look into the street. His dinner was sent him from a neighbouring alehouse, and he opened and shut the shop at a certain hour with his own hands.

His reputation soon extended from one end of the street to the other ; and Mr. Drugget's exemplary conduct was recommended by every master to his apprentice, and by every father to his son. Ned was not only considered as a thriving trader, but as a man of elegance and politeness, for he was remarkably neat in his dress, and would wear his coat threadbare without spotting it ; his hat was always brushed, his shoes glossy his wig nicely curled, and his stockings without a wrinkle. With such qualifications it was not very

difficult for him to gain the heart of Miss Comfit,
the only daughter of Mr. Comfit the confectioner.

Ned is one of those whose happiness marriage
has encreased. His wife had the same disposition
with himself ; and his method of life was very
little changed, except that he dismissed the
lodgers from the first floor, and took the whole
house into his own hands.

He had already, by his parsimony, accumulated
a considerable sum, to which the fortune of his
wife was now added. From this time he began to
grasp at greater acquisitions, and was always ready,
with money in his hand, to pick up the refuse of a
sale, or to buy the stock of a trader who retired
from business. He soon added his parlour to his
shop, and was obliged a few months afterwards to
hire a warehouse.

He had now a shop splendidly and copiously
furnished with every thing that time had injured,
or fashion had degraded, with fragments of tissues,
odd yards of brocade, vast bales of faded silk, and
innumerable boxes of antiquated ribbons. His
shop was soon celebrated through all quarters
of the town, and frequented by every form of
ostentatious poverty. Every maid, whose misfortune it was to be taller than her lady, matched
her gown at Mr. Drugget's ; and many a maiden,
who had passed a winter with her aunt in London,
dazzled the rustics, at her return, with cheap finery
which Drugget had supplied. His shop was often
visited in a morning by ladies who left their
coaches in the next street, and crept through the
alley in linen gowns. Drugget knows the rank

of his customers by their bashfulness; and, when
he finds them unwilling to be seen, invites them
upstairs, or retires with them to the back window.

I rejoiced at the encreasing prosperity of my
friend, and imagined, that as he grew rich, he was
growing happy. His mind has partaken the enlargement of his fortune. When I stepped in for
the first five years, I was welcomed only with a
shake of the hand; in the next period of his life,
he beckoned across the way for a pot of beer; but
for six years past, he invites me to dinner; and if
he bespeaks me the day before, never fails to regale
me with a fillet of veal.

His riches neither made him uncivil nor negligent; he rose at the same hour, attended with the
same assiduity, and bowed with the same gentle-
ness. But for some years he has been much inclined
to talk of the fatigues of business, and the confinement of a shop, and to wish that he had been so
happy as to have renewed his uncle's lease of a
farm, that he might have lived without noise and
hurry, in a pure air, in the artless society of honest
villagers, and the contemplation of the works of
nature.

I soon discovered the cause of my friend's philosophy. He thought himself grown rich enough to
have a lodging in the country, like the mercers on
Ludgate-hill, and was resolved to enjoy himself in
the decline of life. This was a revolution not to
be made suddenly. He talked three years of the
pleasures of the country, but passed every night
over his own shop. But at last he resolved to be
happy, and hired a lodging in the country, that

II   M

he may steal some hours in the week from business; for, says he, *when a man advances in life, he loves to entertain himself sometimes with his own thoughts.*

I was invited to this seat of quiet and contemplation among those whom Mr. Drugget considers as his most reputable friends, and desires to make the first witnesses of his elevation to the highest dignities of a shopkeeper. I found him at Islington,[1] in a room which overlooked the high road, amusing himself with looking through the window, which the clouds of dust would not suffer him to open. He embraced me, told me I was welcome into the country, and asked me, if I did not feel myself refreshed. He then desired that dinner might be hastened, for fresh air always sharpened his appetite, and ordered me a toast and a glass of wine after my walk. He told me much of the pleasure he found in retirement, and wondered what had kept him so long out of the country. After dinner, company came in, and Mr. Drugget again repeated the praises of the country, recommended the pleasures of meditation, and told them, that he had been all the morning at the window, counting the carriages as they passed before him.

[1] Johnson towards the end of his life sometimes went to Islington " for the benefit of good air.'—Boswell's *Johnson,* v. 271.

No. 19. SATURDAY, AUGUST 19, 1758.

SOME of those ancient sages that have exercised their abilities in the inquiry after the *supreme good*, have been of opinion, that the highest degree of earthly happiness is quiet ; a calm repose both of mind and body undisturbed by the sight of folly or the noise of business, the tumults of public commotion, or the agitations of private interest ; a state in which the mind has no other employment, but to observe and regulate her own motions, to trace thought from thought, combine one image with another, raise systems of science and form theories of virtue.

To the scheme of these solitary speculatists, it has been justly objected, that if they are happy, they are happy only by being useless. That mankind is one vast republic,[1] where every individual receives many benefits from the labours of others, which, by labouring in his turn for others, he is obliged to repay ; and that where the united efforts of all are not able to exempt all from misery, none have a right to withdraw from their task of vigilance, or to be indulged in idle wisdom, or solitary pleasures.

It is common for controvertists, in the heat of disputation, to add one position to another till they

[1] See *ante Rambler*, No. 77, where Johnson speaks of " the great republic of humanity."

reach the extremities of knowledge, where truth
and falsehood lose their distinction.   Their admirers follow them to the brink of absurdity, and
then start back from each side towards the middle
point.   So it has happened in this great disquisition.   Many perceive alike the force of the
contrary arguments, find quiet shameful, and
business dangerous, and therefore pass their lives
between them, in bustle without business, and
negligence without quiet.

Among the principal names of this moderate
set is that great philosopher Jack Whirler,[1] whose
business keeps him in perpetual motion, and whose
motion always eludes his business ; who is always
to do what he never does, who cannot stand still
because he is wanted in another place, and who is
wanted in many places because he stays in none.

Jack has more business than he can con-
veniently transact in one house ; he has therefore
one habitation near Bow Church, and another
about a mile distant.   By this ingenious distribution of himself between two houses, Jack has
contrived to be found at neither.   Jack's trade is
extensive, and he has many dealers ; his conversation is sprightly, and he has many companions ;
his disposition is kind, and he has many friends.
Jack neither forbears pleasure for business, nor
omits business for pleasure, but is equally invisible to his friends and his customers ; to him

[1] John Newbery, the bookseller of St. Paul's Churchyard,
was, it is said, the original of Jack Whirler (See *A Bookseller
of the Last Century*, by Charles Welsh, pp. 22, 73).   He
was one of the publishers of the collected edition of *The
Idler*.

that comes with an invitation to a club, and to him that waits to settle an account.

When you call at his house, his clerk tells you, that Mr. Whirler was just stept out, but will be at home exactly at two ; you wait at a coffee-house till two, and then find that he has been at home, and is gone out again, but left word that he should be at the Half-moon-tavern[1] at seven, where he hopes to meet you. At seven you go to the tavern. At eight in comes Mr. Whirler to tell you, that he is glad to see you, and only begs leave to run for a few minutes to a gentleman that lives near the Exchange, from whom he will return before supper can be ready. Away he runs to the Exchange, to tell those who are waiting for him, that he must beg them to defer the business till to-morrow, because his time is come at the Half-moon.

Jack's cheerfulness and civility rank him among those whose presence never gives pain, and whom all receive with fondness and caresses. He calls often on his friends, to tell them, that he will come again to-morrow ; on the morrow he comes again, to tell them how an unexpected summons hurries him away. When he enters a house, his first de-claration is, that he cannot sit down ; and so short are his visits, that he seldom appears to have come for any other reason but to say, He must go.

The dogs of Egypt, when thirst brings them to the Nile, are said to run as they drink for fear of

[1] In Aldersgate-street; " one of Congreve's favourite taverns, the site of which is believed to be marked by Half Moon Passage."—Hutton's *Literary Landmarks of London,* ed. 1888, p. 64.

the crocodiles.   Jack Whirler always dines at full speed.   He enters, finds the family at table, sits familiarly down, and fills his plate ; but while the first morsel is in his mouth, hears the clock strike, and rises ; then goes to another house, sits down again, recollects another engagement; has only time to taste the soup, makes a short excuse to the company, and continues through another street his desultory dinner.

But, overwhelmed as he is with business, his chief desire is to have still more.   Every new proposal takes possession of his thoughts ; he soon balances probabilities, engages in the project, brings it almost to completion, and then forsakes it for another, which he catches with some alacrity, urges with the same vehemence, and abandons with the same coldness.

Every man may be observed to have a certain strain of lamentation, some peculiar theme of complaint on which he dwells in his moments of dejection.   Jack's topic of sorrow is the want of time.   Many an excellent design languishes in empty theory for want of time.   For the omission of any civilities, want of time is his plea to others ; for the neglect of any affairs, want of time is his excuse to himself.   That he wants time, he sincerely believes ; for he once pined away many months with a lingering distemper, for want of time to attend his health.

Thus Jack Whirler lives in perpetual fatigue without proportionate advantage, because he does not consider that no man can see all with his own eyes, or do all with his own hands ; that whoever is engaged in multiplicity of business, must transact much by substitution, and leave something to hazard : and that he who attempts to do all, will waste his life in doing little.

No. 22, SATURDAY, SEPTEMBER 16, 1758.

To the IDLER.

SIR,

S I was passing lately under óne óf the gates of this city, I was struck with horror by a rueful cry, which summoned me *to remember the poor debtors.*

The wisdom and justice of the English laws are by Englishmen at least, loudly celebrated ; but scarcely the most zealous admirers of our institutions can think that law wise, which, when men are capable of work, obliges them to beg ; or just which exposes the liberty of one to the passions of another.

The prosperity of a people is proportionate to the number of hands and minds usefully employed. To the community, sedition is a fever, corruption is a gangrene, and idleness an atrophy. Whatever body, and whatever society, wastes more than it acquires, must gradually decay ; and every being that continues to be fed, and ceases to labour, takes away something from the public stock.

The confinement, therefore, of any man in the sloth and darkness of a prison, is a loss to the nation, and no gain to the creditor. For of the multitudes who are pining in those cells of misery, a very small part is suspected of any fraudulent act, by which they retain what belongs to others. The rest are imprisoned by the wantonness of pride, the malignity of revenge, or the acrimony of disappointed expectation.

If those, who thus rigorously exercise the power which the law has put into their hands, be asked, why they continue to imprison those whom they know to be unable to pay them : one will answer, that his debtor once lived better than himself ; another, that his wife looked above her neighbours, and his children went in silk clothes to the danc-ing school : and another, that he pretended to be a joker and a wit. Some will reply, that if they were in debt, they should meet with the same treatment ; some, that they owe no more than they can pay, and need therefore give no account of their actions. Some will confess their resolution, that their debtors shall rot in jail ; and some will discover, that they hope, by cruelty, to wring the payment from their friends.

The end of all civil regulations is to secure pri-vate happiness from private malignity ; to keep individuals from the power of one another ; but this end is apparently neglected, when a man, irritated with loss, is allowed to be the judge of his own cause, and to assign the punishment of his own pain ; when the distinction between guilt and happiness, between casualty and design, is entrusted to eyes blind with interest, to under-standings depraved by resentment.

Since poverty is punished among us as a crime, it ought at least to be treated with the same lenity as other crimes ; the offender ought not to languish at the will of him whom he has offended, but to be allowed some appeal to the justice of his country. There can be no reason why any debtor should be imprisoned, but that he may be compelled to payment ; and a term should therefore be fixed, in which the creditor should exhibit his accusation of concealed property. If such property can be discovered, let it be given to the creditor ; if the charge is not offered, or cannot be proved, let the prisoner be dismissed.

Those who made the laws have apparently supposed that every deficiency of payment is the crime of the debtor. But the truth is, that the creditor always shares the act, and often more than shares the guilt, of improper trust. It seldom happens that any man imprisons another but for debts which he suffered to be contracted in hope of advantage to himself, and for bargains in which he proportioned his profit to his own opinion of the hazard ; and there is no reason, why one should punish the other for a contract in which both concurred.

Many of the inhabitants of prisons may justly complain of harder treatment. He that once owes more than he can pay, is often obliged to bribe his creditor to patience, by encreasing his debt. Worse and worse commodities, at a higher and higher price, are forced upon him ; he is impoverished by compulsive traffic, and at last overwhelmed, in the common receptacles of misery, by debts, which, without his own consent, were accumulated on his head. To the relief of this distress, no other objection can be made, but that by an easy dissolution of debts fraud will be left without punishment, and imprudence without awe; and that when insolvency should be no longer punishable, credit will cease.

The motive to credit, is the hope of advantage. Commerce can never be at a stop, while one man wants what another can supply; and credit will never be denied, while it is likely to be repaid with profit. He that trusts one whom he designs to sue, is criminal by the act of trust; the cessation of such insidious traffic is to be desired, and no reason can be given why a change of the law should impair any other.

We see nation trade with nation, where no payment can be compelled. Mutual convenience produces mutual confidence; and the merchants continue to satisfy the demands of each other, though they have nothing to dread but the loss of trade.

It is vain to continue an institution, which experience shows to be ineffectual. We have now imprisoned one generation of debtors after another, but we do not find that their numbers lessen. We have now learned, that rashness and imprudence will not be deterred from taking credit; let us try whether fraud and avarice may be more easily restrained from giving it.

I am, SIR, &c.[1]

1 When *The Idlers* were published in volumes this number was substituted for a fable in which war was satirised. See Johnson's *Works*, iv. 450.

No. 27, SATURDAY, OCTOBER 21, 1758.

I T has been the endeavour of all those whom the world has reverenced for superior wisdom, to persuade man to be acquainted with himself, to learn his own powers and his own weakness, to observe by what evils he is most dangerously beset, and by what temptations most easily overcome.

This counsel has been often given with serious dignity, and often received with appearance of conviction ; but as very few can search deep into their own minds without meeting what they wish to hide from themselves, scarcely any man persists in cultivating such disagreeable acquaintance, but draws the veil again between his eyes and his heart, leaves his passions and appetites as he found them, and advises others to look into themselves.

This is the common result of enquiry even among those that endeavour to grow wiser or better : but this endeavour is far enough from frequency ; the greater part of the multitudes that swarm upon the earth have never been disturbed by such uneasy curiosity, but deliver themselves up to business or to pleasure, plunge into the current of life, whether placid or turbulent, and pass on from one point of prospect to another, attentive rather to any thing than the state of their minds ; satisfied, at an easy rate, with an opinion, that they are no worse than others, that every man must mind his own interest, or that their pleasures hurt only themselves, and are therefore no proper subjects of censure.

Some, however, there are, whom the intrusion of scruples, the recollection of better notions, or the latent reprehension of good examples, will not suffer to live entirely contented with their own conduct; these are forced to pacify the mutiny of reason with fair promises, and quiet their thoughts with designs of calling all their actions to review, and planning a new scheme for the time to come.

There is nothing which we estimate so fallaciously as the force of our own resolutions, nor any fallacy which we so unwillingly and tardily detect. He that has resolved a thousand times, and a thousand times deserted his own purpose, yet suffers no abatement of his confidence, but still believes himself his own master; and able by innate vigour of soul, to press forward to his end through all the obstructions that inconveniences or delights can put in his way.

That this mistake should prevail for a time, is very natural. When conviction is present, and temptation out of sight, we do not easily conceive how any reasonable being can deviate from his true interest. What ought to be done while it yet hangs only in speculation, is so plain and certain, that there is no place for doubt; the whole soul yields itself to the predominance of truth, and readily determines to do what, when the time of action comes, will be at last omitted.

I believe most men may review all the lives
that have passed within their observation, without
remembering one efficacious resolution, or being
able to tell a single instance of a course of practice
suddenly changed in consequence of a change of
opinion, or an establishment of determination.[1]
Many indeed, alter their conduct, and are not at
fifty what they were at thirty; but they commonly
varied imperceptibly from themselves, followed
the train of eternal causes, and rather suffered
reformation than made it.

It is not uncommon to charge the difference
between promise and performance, between profession and reality, upon deep design and studied
deceit; but the truth is, that there is very little
hypocrisy in the world;[2] we do not so often

---

[1] Johnson in his *Rasselas*, written a few months later, describes how that prince "passed four months in resolving to
lose no more time in idle resolves."—Ch. iv. On June 1,
1770, he recorded in his *Diary* :—" Every man naturally
persuades himself that he can keep his resolutions, nor is he
convinced of his imbecility but by length of time and frequency of experiment. . . . Those who do not make them are
very few, but of their effect little is perceived ; for scarcely
any man persists in a course of life planned by choice, but
as he is restrained from deviation by some external power.
He who may live as he will seldom lives long in the observation of his own rules."—Boswell's *Johnson*, ii. 114.

[2] When in *Rasselas* (ch. 22) the character of the hermit
was discussed in an assembly of learned men, it was "one of
the youngest among them who with great vehemence pro-
nounced him a hypocrite." According to Reynolds,
Johnson "was not easily imposed upon by professions to
honesty and candour; but he appeared to have little
suspicion of hypocrisy in religion."—Leslie and Taylor's
Life of Reynolds, ii. 459.

endeavour or wish to impose on others as on ourselves; we resolve to do right, we hope to keep our resolutions, we declare them to confirm our own hope, and fix our own inconstancy by calling witnesses of our actions; but at last habit prevails, and those whom we invited to our triumph, laugh at our defeat.

Custom is commonly too strong for the most resolute resolver, though furnished for the assault with all the weapons of philosophy. "He that endeavours to free himself from an ill habit," says Bacon, "must not change too much at a time, "lest he should be discouraged by difficulty; "nor too little, for then he will make but slow "advances."[1] This is a precept which may be applauded in a book, but will fail in the trial, in which every change will be found too great or too little. Those who have been able to conquer habit, are like those that are fabled to have returned from the realms of Pluto:

Pauci, quos æquus amavit
Jupiter, atque ardens evexit ad æthera virtus.[2]

They are sufficient to give hope, but not security; to animate the contest, but not to promise victory.

Those who are in the power of evil habits must conquer them as they can; and conquered they

---

[1] Johnson, I think, quotes from Bacon's essay *Of Nature in Men* (No 38), where it is said:—"He that seeketh victory over his nature let him not set himself too great nor too small tasks; for the first will make him dejected by often failings; and the second will make him a small proceeder, though by often prevailings."

[2] Jupiter, *aut* ardens," etc—*Æneid*, vi. 130.

must be, or neither wisdom nor happiness can be obtained ; but those who are not yet subject to their influence may, by timely caution, preserve their freedom ; they may effectually resolve to escape the tyrant, whom they will very vainly resolve to conquer.

No. 30. SATURDAY, NOVEMBER 11, 1758.

THE desires of man increase with his acquisitions ; every step which he advances brings something within his view, which he did not see before, and which, as soon as he sees it, he begins to want. Where necessity ends, curiosity begins ; and no sooner are we supplied with every thing that nature can demand, than we sit down to contrive artificial appetites

By this restlessness of mind, every populous and wealthy city is filled with innumerable employments, for which the greater part of mankind is without a name : with artificers, whose labour is exerted in producing such petty conveniences, that many shops are furnished with instruments, of which the use can hardly be found without enquiry, but which he that once knows them quickly learns to number among necessary things.

Such is the diligence with which, in countries completely civilized, one part of mankind labours for another, that wants are supplied faster than they can be formed, and the idle and luxurious find life stagnate for want of some desire to keep it in motion. ·This species of distress furnishes a new set of occupations ; and multitudes are busied, from day to day, in finding the rich and the fortunate something to do.

It is very common to reproach those artists as useless, who produce only such superfluities as neither accommodate the body nor improve the mind ; and of which no other effect can be imagined, than that they are the occasions of spending money, and consuming time.

But this censure will be mitigated, when it is seriously considered, that money and time are the heaviest burdens of life, and that the unhappiest of all mortals are those who have more of either than they know how to use. To set himself free from these incumbrances, one hurries to Newmarket ; another travels over Europe ; one pulls down his house and calls architects about him ; another buys a seat in the country, and follows his hounds over hedges and through rivers ; one makes collections of shells ; and another searches the world for tulips and carnations.

He is surely a public benefactor who finds employment for those to whom it is thus difficult to find it for themselves. It is true, that this is seldom done merely from generosity or compassion ; almost every man seeks his own advantage in helping others, and therefore it is too common for mercenary officiousness to consider rather what is grateful than what is right.

We all know that it is more profitable to be loved than esteemed; and ministers of pleasure will always be found, who study to make themselves necessary, and to supplant those who are practising the same arts.

One of the amusements of idleness is reading without the fatigue of close attention, and the world therefore swarms with writers whose wish is not to be studied, but to be read.

No species of literary men has lately been so much multiplied as the writers of news. Not many years ago the nation was content with one gazette; but now we have not only in the metropolis papers for every morning and every evening, but almost every large town has its weekly historian,[1] who regularly circulates his periodical intelligence, and fills the villages of his district with conjectures on the event of war, and with debates on the true interests of Europe.

To write news in its perfection requires such a combination of qualities, that a man completely fitted for the task is not always to be found. In Sir Henry Wotton's jocular definition, *An ambassador* is said to be *a man of virtue sent abroad to tell lies for the advantage of his country;*[2] a

[1] The *Birmingham Journal*, for which Johnson wrote some essays, was started in 1732.—Boswell's *Johnson*, i. 85.

[2] Wotton, passing through Germany on his way to Venice as ambassador, wrote in an album the following "pleasant definition:—*Legatus est vir bonus, peregre missus ad mentiendum Reipublicæ causa.* Which he could have been content should have been thus Englished:—*An Am-*

news-writer is *a man without virtue, who writes lies at home for his own profit.* To these compositions is required neither genius nor knowledge, neither industry nor sprightliness ; but contempt of shame and indifference to truth are absolutely necessary. He who by a long familiarity with infamy has obtained these qualities, may confidently tell to-day what he intends to contradict to-morrow ; he may affirm fearlessly what he knows that he shall be obliged to recant, and may write letters from Amsterdam or Dresden to himself.

In a time of war the nation is always of one mind, eager to hear something good of themselves and ill of the enemy. At this time the task of news-writers is easy: they have nothing to do but to tell that a battle is expected, and afterwards that a battle has been fought, in which we and our friends, whether conquering or conquered, did all, and our enemies did nothing.

Scarcely any thing awakens attention like a tale of cruelty. The writer of news never fails in the

---

bassador is an honest man, sent to lie abroad for the good of his country. But the word for lie—being the hinge upon which the conceit was to turn—was not so expressed in Latin as would admit—in the hands of an enemy especially—so fair a construction as Sir Henry thought in English." This pleasantry brought him into some trouble, being used against him and the English Court by "Scioppius, a Romanist, a man of a restless spirit and a malicious pen."—Walton's *Lives*, ed. 1838, p. 123. Dryden, referring to this story, says :— "Sure a poet is as much privileged to lie as an ambassador, for the honour and interest of his country."—Dryden's *Works*, xiv. 175.

intermission of action to tell how the enemies murdered children and ravished virgins ; and, if the scene of action be somewhat distant, scalps half the inhabitants of a province.

Among the calamities of war may be justly numbered the diminution of the love of truth, by the falsehoods which interest dictates, and credulity encourages. A peace will equally leave the warrior and relator of wars destitute of employment ; and I know not whether more is to be dreaded from streets filled with soldiers accustomed to plunder, or from garrets filled with scribblers accustomed to lie.[1]

No. 31. SATURDAY, NOVEMBER 18, 1758.

ANY moralists have remarked, that pride has of all human vices the widest dominion, appears in the greatest multiplicity of forms, and lies hid under the greatest variety of disguises ; of disguises, which, like the moon's *veil of brightness*,

---

[1] With this attack on the writers of news we may compare the discussion in which Johnson, speaking of the ancient Greeks and Romans, said :—" Sir, the mass of both of them were barbarians. The mass of every people must be barbarous where there is no printing, and consequently knowledge is not generally diffused. Knowledge is diffused among our people by the newspapers."—Boswell's *Johnson,* ii. 170.

are both its *lustre and its shade*,[1] and betray it to others, though they hide it from ourselves.

It is not my intention to degrade pride from this pre-eminence of mischief; yet I know not whether idleness may not maintain a very doubtful and obstinate competition.

There are some that profess idleness in its full dignity, who call themselves the *Idle*, as *Busiris* in the play *calls himself the proud ;*[2] who boast that they do nothing, and thank their stars that they have nothing to do ; who sleep every night till they can sleep no longer, and rise only that exercise may enable them to sleep again ; who prolong the reign of darkness by double curtains, and never see the sun but to *tell him how they hate his beams ;*[3] whose whole labour is to vary the posture of indulgence, and whose day differs from their night but as a couch or chair differs from a bed.

These are the true and open votaries of idleness, for whom she weaves the garlands of poppies, and into whose cup she pours the waters of oblivion ; who exist in a state of unruffled

[1] " The moon pull'd off her veil of light,
     That hides her face by day from sight,
     (Mysterious veil, of brightness made,
     That's both her lustre and her shade)
     And in the lanthorn of the night,
     With shining horns hung out her light."
                              —*Hudibras*, ii. 1, 905.
[2] " He calls himself The Proud, and glories in it."
                    —Dr. Young, *Busiris*, act i. l. 14.
[3]   to thee I call,
     " But with no friendly voice, and add thy name,
     O Sun, to tell thee how I hate thy beams."
                              —*Paradise Lost*, iv. 35.

stupidity, forgetting and forgotten ; who have long ceased to live, and at whose death the sur-vivors can only say, that they have ceased to breathe.

But idleness predominates in many lives where it is not suspected ; for, being a vice which termi-nates in itself, it may be enjoyed without injury to others ; and it is therefore not watched like fraud, which endangers property ; or like pride, which naturally seeks its gratifications in another's inferiority. Idleness is a silent and peaceful quality, that neither raises envy by ostentation, nor hatred by opposition ; and therefore nobody is busy to censure or detect it.

As pride sometimes is hid under humility, idle-ness is often covered by turbulence and hurry. He that neglects his known duty and real employ-ment, naturally endeavours to crowd his mind with something that may bar out the remembrance of his own folly, and does any thing but what he ought to do with eager diligence, that he may keep himself in his own favour.

Some are always in a state of preparation, occupied in previous measures, forming plans, accumulating materials, and providing for the main affair. These are certainly under the secret power of idleness. Nothing is to be expected from the workman whose tools are for ever to be sought. I was once told by a great master,[1] that no man ever excelled in painting, who was eminently curious about pencils and colours.

There are others to whom idleness dictates

[1] Johnson knew Hogarth and Reynolds.

another expedient, by which life may be passed
unprofitably away without the tediousness of many
vacant hours.   The art is, to fill the day with
petty business, to have always something in hand
which may raise curiosity, but not solicitude, and
keep the mind in a state of action, but not of
labour.

This art has for many years been practised by
my old friend Sober[1] with wonderful success.
Sober is a man of strong desires and quick
imagination, so exactly balanced by the love of
ease, that they can seldom stimulate him to any
difficult undertaking ; they have, however, so
much power, that they will not suffer him to lie
quite at rest ; and though they do not make him
sufficiently useful to others, they make him at
least weary of himself.

Mr. Sober's chief pleasure is conversation ;
there is no end of his talk or his attention ; to
speak or to hear is equally pleasing ; for he still
fancies that he is teaching or learning something,
and is free for the time from his own reproaches.

But there is one time at night when he must go
home, that his friends may sleep ; and another
time in the morning, when all the world agrees to
shut out interruption.   These are the moments of
which poor Sober trembles at the thought.[2]   But

[1] " Mr. Johnson told me that the character of Sober in *The
Idler* was by himself intended as his own portrait."—Piozzi's
Anecdotes, p. 48.

[2] " Solitude," wrote Reynolds, " to Johnson was horror ;
nor would he ever trust himself alone but when employed
in writing or reading.   He has often begged me to go home
with him to prevent his being alone in the coach."—Boswell's

the misery of these tiresome intervals he has
many means of alleviating. He has persuaded
himself, that the manual arts are undeservedly
overlooked ; he has observed in many trades the
effects of close thought, and just ratiocination.
From speculation he proceeded to practice, and
supplied himself with the tools of a carpenter, with
which he mended his coal-box very successfully,
and which he still continues to employ, as he
finds occasion.

He has attempted at other times the crafts of
the shoemaker, tinman, plumber, and potter ; in
all these arts he has failed, and resolves to qualify
himself for them by better information. But his
daily amusement is chemistry. He has a small
furnace, which he employs in distillation, and
which has long been the·solace of his life.[1] He
draws oils and waters, and essences, and spirits,
which he knows to be of no use ; sits and counts

Johnson, i. 144, *n.* 2. Dr. Burney describes the "many long
conversations" which he and Johnson had at Streatham, "often
sitting up as long as the fire and candles lasted, and much
longer than the patience of the servants subsisted."—*Ib.* ii. 406.
"Whoever thinks of going to bed before twelve o'clock is
(Johnson said) a scoundrel."—*Ib.* iii., 1, *n.* 1.

[1] "Dr. Johnson sometimes employed himself in chemistry,
sometimes in watering and pruning a vine, sometimes in
small experiments, at which those who may smile should
recollect that there are moments which admit of being soothed
only by trifles."—*Ib.* iii.,398. "We made up a sort of laboratory at Streatham one summer. But the danger Mr. Thrale
found his friend in one day, when he got the children and
servants round him to see some experiments performed, put
an end to all our entertainment."—Piozzi's *Anecdotes*, p.
236.

the drops as they come from his retort, and forgets
that, whilst a drop is falling, a moment flies away.

Poor Sober! I have often teazed him with reproof, and he has often promised reformation ; for
no man is so much open to conviction as the *Idler*,
but there is none on whom it operates so little.
What will be the effect of this paper I know not ;
perhaps he will read it and laugh, and light the
fire in his furnace ; but my hope is, that he will
quit his trifles, and betake himself to rational and
useful diligence.

No. 38, SATURDAY, JANUARY 6, 1759.

SINCE the publication of the letter concerning the condition of those who are
confined in gaols by their creditors, an
inquiry is said to have been made, by
which it appears that more than twenty thousand[1]
are at this time prisoners for debt.

We often look with indifference on the successive parts of that, which, if the whole were seen
together, would shake us with emotion. A debtor
is dragged to prison, pitied for a moment, and
then forgotten ; another follows him, and is lost
alike in the caverns of oblivion ; but when the
whole mass of calamity rises up at once, when
twenty thousand reasonable beings are heard
all groaning in unnecessary misery, not by the

[1] This number was at that time confidently published ; but
the author has since found reason to question the calculation.

infirmity of nature, but the mistake or negligence of policy, who can forbear to pity and lament, to wonder and abhor!

There is here no need of declamatory vehemence; we live in an age of commerce and computation; let us therefore coolly enquire what is the sum of evil which the imprisonment of debtors brings upon our country.

It seems to be the opinion of the later computists, that the inhabitants of England do not exceed six millions, of which twenty thousand is the three-hundredth part. What shall we say of the humanity or the wisdom of a nation that voluntarily sacrifices one in every three hundred to lingering destruction!

The misfortunes of an individual do not extend their influence to many; yet if we consider the effects of consanguinity and friendship, and the general reciprocation of wants and benefits, which make one man dear or necessary to another, it may reasonably be supposed, that every man languishing in prison gives trouble of some kind to two others who love or need him. By this multiplication of misery we see distress extended to the hundredth part of the whole society.

If we estimate at a shilling a day what is lost by the inaction and consumed in the support of each man thus chained down to involuntary idleness, the public loss will rise in one year to three hundred thousand pounds; in ten years to more than a sixth part of our circulating coin.

I am afraid that those who are best acquainted

with the state of our prisons will confess that
my conjecture is too near the truth, when I
suppose that the corrosion of resentment, the
heaviness of sorrow, the corruption of confined
air, the want of exercise, and sometimes of food,[1]
the contagion of diseases, from which there is no
retreat, and the severity of tyrants,[2] against whom
there can be no resistance, and all the complicated horrors of prison, put an end every year
to the life of one in four of those that are shut
up from the common comforts of human life.

Thus perish yearly five thousand men, over-

[1] John Howard, writing of debtors' side of the prison in
York Castle, describes it, so far as buildings go, as "a noble
prison which does honour to the country." He adds that " the
allowance for prisoners, whether debtors or felons, was a sixpenny loaf each on *Tuesday* and *Friday* " (weight in Novem-
ber, 1774, 3 lb. 2 oz). There were confined on Jan. 25 of
that year 110 debtors.—*State of the Prisons in England
and Wales*, ed. 1777, p. 396. Speaking of the general
allowance of bread, he says:—"It is probable that when it
was fixed by its value near double the quantity that the
money will now purchase might be bought for it ; yet the
allowance continues unaltered . . . In some prisons many
criminals are half-starved ; such of them as at their commit-
ment were in health come out almost famished, scarce able to
move, and for weeks incapable of any labour."—*Ib.*, p. 12.   If
many criminals, so also some debtors must have been half-
starved, as the allowance of food was the same for both classes.

[2] Johnson, in his *Life of Savage*, praising the keeper of the
Bristol gaol, had said :—"Virtue is undoubtedly most
laudable in that state which makes it most difficult ;
and, therefore, the humanity of a gaoler certainly deserves
this public attestation."—Johnson's *Works*, viii. 183.   Fielding, in the opening chapters of his *Amelia*, "discloses
the secrets of the prison-house," and the brutality of the
ruffian who was the keeper.

borne with sorrow, consumed by famine, or putrified by filth; many of them in the most vigorous and useful part of life; for the thoughtless and imprudent are commonly young, and the active and busy are seldom old.

According to the rule generally received, which supposes that one in thirty dies yearly, the race of man may be said to be renewed at the end of thirty years. Who would have believed till now, that of every English generation, an hundred and fifty thousand perish in our gaols! that in every century, a nation eminent for science, studious of commerce, ambitious of empire, should willingly lose, in noisome dungeons, five hundred thousand of its inhabitants; a number greater than has ever been destroyed in the same time by the pestilence and sword!

A very late occurrence may show us the value of the number which we thus condemn to be useless; in the re-establishment of the trained bands, thirty thousand are considered as a force sufficient against all exigencies.[1] While, therefore, we detain twenty thousand in prison, we shut up in darkness and uselessness two-thirds of an army which ourselves judge equal to the defence of our country.

The monastic institutions have been often blamed, as tending to retard the increase of

[1] In 1757 a Bill had been passed for establishing the militia. "Johnson was once drawn to serve in the militia, the Trained Bands of the City of London. . . . He provided himself with a musket and with a sword and belt, which I have seen hanging in his closet."—Boswell's *Johnson*, iv. 319.

mankind. And perhaps retirement ought rarely to be permitted, except to those whose employment is consistent with abstraction, and who, though solitary, will not be idle; to those whom infirmity makes useless to the commonwealth, or to those who have paid their due proportion to society, and who, having lived for others, may be honourably dismissed to live for themselves.[1] But whatever be the evil or the folly of these retreats, those have no right to censure them whose prisons contain greater numbers than the monasteries of other countries. It is, surely, less foolish and less criminal to permit inaction than compel it; to comply with doubtful opinions of happiness, than condemn to certain and apparent misery; to indulge the extravagances of erroneous piety, than to multiply and enforce temptations to wickedness.

The misery of gaols is not half their evil: they are filled with every corruption which poverty and wickedness can generate between them; with all the shameless and profligate enormities that can be produced by the impudence of ignominy, the rage of want, and the malignity of despair. In a prison the awe of the public eye is lost, and the power of the law is spent; there are few fears, there are no blushes.

1 "Johnson said, 'If convents should be allowed at all, they should only be retreats for persons unable to serve the public, or who have served it. It is our first duty to serve society, and, after we have done that, we may attend wholly to the salvation of our own souls. A youthful passion for abstracted devotion should not be encouraged.'" — Boswell's *Johnson*, ii. 10.

The lewd inflame the lewd, the audacious harden the audacious. Every one fortifies himself as he can against his own sensibility, endeavours to practise on others the arts which are practised on himself; and gains the kindness of his associates by similitude of manners.[1]

Thus some sink amidst their misery, and others survive only to propagate villainy. It may be hoped, that our lawgivers will at length take away from us this power of starving and depraving one another; but, if there be any reason why this inveterate evil should not be removed in our age, which true policy has enlightened beyond any former time, let those, whose writings form the opinions and the practices of their contemporaries, endeavour to transfer the reproach of such imprisonment from the debtor to the creditor, till universal infamy shall pursue the wretch whose wantonness of power, or revenge of disappointment, condemns another to torture and to ruin; till he shall be hunted through the world as an enemy to man, and find in riches no shelter from contempt.

1 John Howard, in his *State of the Prisons in England and Wales*, ed. 1777, p. 24, quotes this paragraph. John Wesley recorded on Feb. 3, 1753 :—".I visited one in the Marshalsea prison, a nursery of all manner of wickedness. O shame to man, that there should be such a place, such a picture of hell upon earth !" A few days later he wrote :—" I visited as many more as I could. I found some in their cells underground ; others in their garrets, half starved both with cold and hunger, added to weakness and pain."—Wesley's *Journal*, ed. 1827, ii. 267.

Surely, he whose debtor has perished in prison, although he may acquit himself of deliberate murder, must at least have. his mind clouded with discontent, when he considers how much another has suffered from him; when he thinks on the wife bewailing her husband, or the children begging the bread which their father would have earned. If there are any made so obdurate by avarice or cruelty, as to revolve these consequences without dread or pity, I must leave them to be awakened by some other power, for I write only to human beings.[1]

[1] Three years earlier Johnson had been in danger of a debtor's prison himself, being " under an arrest for five pounds eighteen shillings." He was freed by a loan from Richardson, the novelist.—Boswell's *Johnson*, i. 304.

No. 41, SATURDAY, JANUARY 27, 1759.

HE following letter relates to an affliction perhaps not necessary to be
imparted to the public;[1] but I could
not persuade myself to suppress it,
because I think I know the sentiments to be
sincere, and I feel no disposition to provide for
this day any other entertainment.

> *At tu quisquis eris, miseri qui cruda poetæ*
> *Credideris fletu funera digna tuo,*
> *Hæc postrema tibi sit flendi causa, fluatque*
> *Lenis inoffenso vitaque morsque gradu.*

MR. IDLER,

OTWITHSTANDING the warnings of
philosophers, and the daily examples
of losses and misfortunes which life
forces upon our observation, such is
the absorption of our thoughts in the business
of the present day, such the resignation of our
reason to empty hopes of future felicity, or such
our unwillingness to foresee what we dread, that
every calamity comes suddenly upon us, and not

---

[1] He had just lost his mother, who died on the 20th or 21st
of January at the great age of ninety.—Boswell's *Johnson*, i.
339, 514. As soon as he heard of her illness he began to write
Rasselas, so that he might have money in readiness. With
it he paid her debts and funeral expenses. He composed it
in the evenings of one week, and had finished it, it should
seem, on January 22.—*Rasselas*, Clarendon Press edition,
p. 22.

only presses us as a burden, but crushes as a blow.

There are evils which happen out of the common course of nature, against which it is no reproach not to be provided. A flash of lightning intercepts the traveller in his way. The concussion of an earthquake heaps the ruins of cities upon their inhabitants. But other miseries time brings, though silently yet visibly, forward by its even lapse, which yet approach us unseen because we turn our eyes away, and seize us unresisted because we could not arm ourselves against them but by setting them before us.

That it is vain to shrink from what cannot be avoided, and to hide that from ourselves which must some time be found, is a truth which we all know, but which all neglect, and perhaps none more than the speculative reasoner, whose thoughts are always from home, whose eye wanders over life, whose fancy dances after meteors of happiness kindled by itself, and who examines every thing rather than his own state.

Nothing is more evident than that the decays of age must terminate in death ; yet there is no man, says Tully, who does not believe that he may yet live another year ;[1] and there is none who does not, upon the same principle, hope another year for his parent or his friend : but the fallacy will be in time detected ; the last

[1] See *ante*, *The Adventurer*, No. 69.

year, the last day, must come. It has come
and is past. The life which made my own life
pleasant is at an end, and the gates of death
are shut upon my prospects.

The loss of a friend upon whom the heart was
fixed, to whom every wish and endeavour tended,
is a state of dreary desolation, in which the
mind looks abroad impatient of itself, and finds
nothing but emptiness and horror. The blame-
less life, the artless tenderness, the pious simplicity, the modest resignation, the patient
sickness, and the quiet death, are remembered
only to add value to the loss, to aggravate regret
for what cannot be amended, to deepen sorrow
for what cannot be recalled.

These are the calamities by which Providence
gradually disengages us from the love of life.
Other evils fortitude may repel, or hope may
mitigate ; but irreparable privation leaves nothing
to exercise resolution or flatter expectation. The
dead cannot return, and nothing is left us here
but languishment and grief.

Yet such is the course of nature, that whoever
lives long must outlive those whom he loves and
honours. Such is the condition of our present
existence, that life must one time lose its associa-
tions, and every inhabitant of the earth must
walk downward to the grave alone and unre-
garded, without any partner of his joy or grief,
without any interested witness of his misfortunes or success.

Misfortune, indeed, he may yet feel ; for where
is the bottom of the misery of man ? But what is

success to him that has none to enjoy it ?[1]   Happiness is not found in self-contemplation ; it is perceived only when it is reflected from another.

We know little of the state of departed souls, because such knowledge is not necessary to a good life.[2]   Reason deserts us at the brink of the grave, and can give no further intelligence.   Revelation is not wholly silent.   *There is joy in the angels of heaven over one sinner that repenteth ;* and surely this joy is not incommunicable to souls disentangled from the body, and made like angels.

Let hope therefore dictate, what revelation does not confute, that the union of souls may still remain ; and that we who are struggling with sin, sorrow, and infirmities, may have our part in the attention and kindness of those who have finished their course, and are now receiving their reward.

These are the great occasions which force the

---

[1] He had expressed the same feeling four years earlier in his letter to Lord Chesterfield :—"I am solitary and cannot impart it."   There he was thinking of the loss of his wife.   In his *Rasselas*, ch. 45, he makes a sage say with a sigh :— " Praise is to an old man an empty sound.   I have neither mother to be delighted with the reputation of her son, nor wife to partake the honours of her husband."

[2] " That Johnson, in conformity with the opinion of many of the most able, learned, and pious Christians, in all ages, supposed that there was a middle state after death, previous to the time at which departed souls are finally received to eternal felicity, appears, I think, unquestionably from his devotions."—Boswell's *Johnson*, i. 240.   On Easter Day, 1764, he recorded in his *Diary* :—"After sermon I recommended *T*etty [his wife] in a prayer by herself ; and my father, mother, brother, and Bathurst in another.   I did it only once, so far as it might be lawful for me."—*Prayers and Meditations*, p. 54.

mind to take refuge in religion : when we have no help in ourselves, what can remain but that we look up to a higher and a greater Power? and to what hope may we not raise our eyes and hearts, when we consider that the greatest POWER is the BEST ?[1]

Surely there is no man who, thus afflicted, does not seek succour in the *gospel*, which has brought *life and immortality to light*.[2] The precepts of *Epicurus*, who teaches us to endure what the laws of the universe make necessary, may silence, but not content us. The dictates of *Zeno*, who commands us to look with indifference on external things, may dispose us to conceal our sorrow, but cannot assuage it. Real alleviation for the loss of friends, and rational tranquillity in the prospect of our own dissolution, can be received only from the promises of Him in whose hands are life and death, and from the assurance of another and better state, in which all tears shall be wiped from the eyes, and the whole soul shall be filled with joy. Philosophy may infuse stubbornness, but Religion only can give patience.

I am, &c.

[1] "Where then shall hope and fear their objects find ?
Must dull suspense corrupt the stagnant mind ?
Must helpless man in ignorance sedate
Roll darkling down the torrent of his fate ?
Must no dislike alarm, no wishes rise,
No cries invoke the mercies of the skies ?
Inquirer, cease ; petitions yet remain,
Which heaven may hear ; nor deem religion vain."
—*The Vanity of Human Wishes*, l. 343.

[2] 2 *Timothy*, i. 10.

No. 48. SATURDAY, MARCH 17, 1759.

THERE is no kind of idleness, by which we are so easily seduced, as that which dignifies itself by the appearance of business, and by making the loiterer imagine that he has something to do which must not be neglected, keeps him in perpetual agitation, and hurries him rapidly from place to place.

He that sits still, or reposes himself upon a couch, no more deceives himself than he deceives others ; he knows that he is doing nothing, and has no other solace of his insignificance than the resolution, which the lazy hourly make, of changing his mode of life.

To do nothing every man is ashamed : and to do much almost every man is unwilling or afraid. Innumerable expedients have therefore been invented to produce motion without labour, and employment without solicitude. The greater part of those whom the kindness of fortune has left to their own direction, and whom want does not keep chained to the counter or the plough, play throughout life with the shadows of business, and know not at last what they have been doing.

These imitators of action are of all denominations. Some are seen at every auction without intention to purchase ; others appear punctually at the Exchange, though they are known there only by their faces. Some are always making parties to visit collections for which they have no taste ; and some neglect every pleasure and every duty to hear questions, in which they have no interest, debated in parliament.

These men never appear more ridiculous than in the distress which they imagine themselves to feel, from some accidental interruption of those empty pursuits. A tyger newly imprisoned is indeed more formidable, but not more angry, than Jack Tulip withheld from a florist's feast, or Tom Distich hindered from seeing the first representation of a play.

As political affairs are the highest and most extensive of temporal concerns, the mimic of a politician is more busy and important than any other trifler. Monsieur le Noir, a man who, without property or importance in any corner of the earth, has, in the present confusion of the world, declared himself a steady adherent to the French, is made miserable by a wind that keeps back the packet-boat, and still more miserable by every account of a Malouin privateer[1] caught in his cruize ; he knows well that nothing can be done or said by him which can produce any effect but that of laughter, that he can neither hasten nor retard good or evil, that his joys and sorrows have scarcely any partakers ; yet such is his zeal, and such his curiosity, that he would run barefooted to Gravesend, for the sake of knowing first that the English had lost a tender, and would ride out to meet every mail from the continent if he might be permitted to open it.

Learning is generally confessed to be desirable,

[1] A privateer of St. Malo.

and there are some who fancy themselves always busy in acquiring it. Of these ambulatory students, one of the most busy is my friend **Tom Restless.**[1]

Tom has long had a mind to be a man of knowledge, but he does not care to spend much time among authors ; for he is of opinion that few books deserve the labour of perusal, that they give the mind an unfashionable cast, and destroy that freedom of thought and easiness of manners indispensably requisite to acceptance in the world. Tom has therefore found another way to wisdom. When he rises he goes into a coffee-house, where he creeps so near to men whom he takes to be reasoners as to hear their discourse, and endeavours to remember something which, when it has been strained through Tom's head, is so near to nothing, that what it once was cannot be discovered. This he carries round from friend to friend through a circle of visits, till, hearing what each says upon the question, he becomes able at dinner to say a little himself ; and, as every great genius relaxes himself among his inferiors, meets with some who wonder how so young a man can talk so wisely.

At night he has a new feast prepared for his intellects ; he always runs to a disputing society, or a speaking club, where he half hears what, if he

---

1 Tom Restless was meant for Mr. Thomas Tyers ; "a circumstance," says Mr. Nichols, "pointed out to me by Dr. Johnson himself." He wrote a biographical sketch of Johnson. Boswell describes him as a man who "ran about the world with a pleasant carelessness, amusing everybody by his desultory conversation."—Boswell's *Johnson*, iii. 308.

had heard the whole, he would but half understand ; goes home pleased with the consciousness of a day well spent, lies down full of ideas, and rises in the morning empty as before.

No. 57. SATURDAY, MAY 19, 1759.

PRUDENCE is of more frequent use than any other intellectual quality ; it is exerted on slight occasions, and called into act by the cursory business of common life.

Whatever is universally necessary, has been granted to mankind on easy terms. Prudence, as it is always wanted, is without great difficulty obtained. It requires neither extensive nor profound search, but forces itself, by spontaneous impulse, upon a mind neither great nor busy, neither engrossed by vast designs, nor distracted by multiplicity of attention.

Prudence operates on life in the same manner as rules on composition : it produces vigilance rather than elevation, rather prevents loss than procures advantage ; and often escapes miscarriages but seldom reaches either power or honour. It quenches that ardour of enterprize, by which everything is done that can claim praise or admiration ; and represses that generous temerity which often fails and often succeeds. Rules may obviate faults, but can never confer beauties ; and prudence keeps life safe, but does not often make it happy.

The world is not amazed with prodigies of excellence, but when wit tramples upon rules, and
magnanimity breaks the chains of prudence.

One of the most prudent of all that have fallen
within my observation, is my old companion Sophron, who has passed through the world in quiet, by
perpetual adherence to a few plain maxims, and
wonders how contention and distress can so often
happen.

The first principle of Sophron is to *run no
hazards.* Though he loves money, he is of opinion,
that frugality is a more certain source of riches
than industry. It is to no purpose that any
prospect of large profit is set before him; he
believes little about futurity, and does not love to
trust his money out of his sight, for nobody knows
what may happen. He has a small estate, which
he lets at the old rent, because *it is better to have a
little than nothing;* but he rigorously demands
payment on the stated day, for *he that cannot pay
one quarter cannot pay two.* If he is told of any
improvements in agriculture, he likes the old way,
has observed that changes very seldom answer
expectation, is of opinion that our forefathers knew
how to till the ground as well as we ; and concludes
with an argument that nothing can over-power
that the expence of planting and fencing is immediate, and the advantage distant, and that *he
is no wise man that will quit a certainty for an
uncertainty.*

Another of Sophron's rules is, *to mind no business
but his own.* In the state he is of no party ; but
hears and speaks of public affairs with the same

coldness as of the administration of same ancient republic. If any flagrant act of fraud or oppression is mentioned, he hopes that *all is not true that is told* : if misconduct or corruption puts the nation in a flame, he hopes that *every man means well.* At elections he leaves his dependants to their own choice, and declines to vote himself, for every candidate is a good man, whom he is unwilling to oppose or offend.

If disputes happen among his neighbours, he observes an invariable and cold neutrality. His punctuality has gained him the reputation of honesty, and his caution that of wisdom ; and few would refuse to refer their claims to his award. He might have prevented many expensive lawsuits, and quenched many a feud in its first smoke ; but always refuses the office of arbitration, because he must decide against one or the other.

With the affairs of other families he is always unacquainted. He sees estates bought and sold, squandered and increased, without praising the economist, or censuring the spendthrift. He never courts the rising, lest they should fall ; nor insults the fallen, lest they should rise again. His caution has the appearance of virtue, and all who do not want his help praise his benevolence ; but if any man solicits his assistance, he has just sent away all his money ; and, when the petitioner is gone, declares to his family that he is sorry for his misfortunes, has always looked upon him with particular kindness, and therefore could not lend him money, lest he should destroy their friendship by the necessity of enforcing payment.

Of domestic misfortunes he has never heard. When he is told the hundredth time of a gentleman's daughter who has married the coachman, he lifts up his hands with astonishment, for he always thought her a very sober girl. When nuptial quarrels, after having filled the country with talk and laughter, at least end in separation, he never can conceive how it happened, for he looked upon them as a happy couple.

If his advice is asked he never gives any particular direction, because events are uncertain, and he will bring no blame upon himself; but he takes the consulter tenderly by the hand, tells him he makes his case his own, and advises him not to act rashly, but to weigh the reasons on both sides; observes, that a man may be as easily too hasty as too slow, and that as many fail by doing too much as too little; that *a wise man has two ears and one tongue;* and *that little said is soon mended;* that he could tell him this and that, but that after all every man is the best judge of his own affairs.

With this some are satisfied, and go home with great reverence of Sophron's wisdom; and none are offended, because every one is left in full possession of his own opinion.

Sophron gives no characters. It is equally vain to tell him of vice and virtue; for he has remarked, that no man likes to be censured, and that very few are delighted with the praises of another. He has a few terms which he uses to all alike. With respect to fortune, he believes every family to be in good circumstances; he never exalts any understanding by lavish praise, yet he meets with none but very sensible people. Every man is honest and hearty; and every woman is a good creature.

Thus Sophron creeps along, neither loved nor hated, neither favoured nor opposed: he has never attempted to grow rich, for fear of growing poor; and has raised no friends, for fear of making enemies.

No. 58. SATURDAY, MAY 26, 1759.

PLEASURE is very seldom found where it is sought. Our brightest blazes of gladness are commonly kindled by unexpected sparks. The flowers which scatter their odours from time to time in the paths of life, grow up without culture from seeds scattered by chance.

Nothing is more hopeless than a scheme of merriment.[1] Wits and humourists are brought together from distant quarters by preconcerted invitations; they come attended by their admirers prepared to laugh and to applaud; they gaze a-while on each other, ashamed to be silent, and afraid to speak; every man is discontented with himself, grows angry with those that give him pain, and resolves that he will contribute nothing

[1] Johnson, writing to Mrs. Thrale, said:—"That the regatta disappointed you is neither wonderful nor new; all pleasure preconceived and preconcerted ends in disappointment."—*Piozzi Letters*, i. 255.

to the merriment of such worthless company. Wine inflames the general malignity, and changes sullenness to petulance, till at last none can bear any longer the presence of the rest.   They retire to vent their indignation in safer places, where they are heard with attention ; their importance is restored, they recover their good humour, and gladden the night with wit and jocularity.

Merriment is always the effect of a sudden impression.   The jest which is expected is already destroyed.   The most active imagination will be sometimes torpid under the frigid influence of melancholy, and sometimes occasions will be wanting to tempt the mind, however volatile, to sallies and excursions.   Nothing was ever said with uncommon felicity, but by the co-operation of chance; and, therefore, wit as well as valour must be content to share its honours with fortune.

All other pleasures are equally uncertain ; the general remedy of uneasiness is change of place ; almost every one has some journey of pleasure in his mind, with which he flatters his expectation. He that travels in theory has no inconvenience ; he has shade and sunshine at his disposal, and wherever he alights finds tables of plenty and looks of gaiety.   These ideas are indulged till the day of departure arrives, the chaise is called, and the progress of happiness begins.

A few miles teach him the fallacies of imagination.   The road is dusty, the air is sultry, the horses are sluggish, and the postilion brutal.   He longs for the time of dinner, that he may eat and rest.[1] The inn is crowded, his orders are neglected, and nothing remains but that he devour in haste what the cook has spoiled, and drive on in quest of better entertainment. He finds at night a more commodious house, but the best is always worse than he expected.[2]

He at last enters his native province, and resolves to feast his mind with the conversation of his old friends, and the recollection of juvenile frolics. He stops at the house of his friend, whom he designs to overpower with pleasure by the unexpected interview. He is not known till he tells his name, and revives the memory of himself by a gradual explanation. He is then coldly received, and ceremoniously feasted. He hastes away to another, whom his affairs have called to a distant place, and, having seen the empty house, goes away disgusted, by a disappointment which could not be intended because it could not be foreseen. At the next house he finds every face clouded with misfortune, and is regarded with malevolence as an unreasonable intruder, who comes not to visit but to insult them.

It is seldom that we find either men or places

[1] When Johnson became rich enough to travel luxuriously he expressed himself very differently. "As we were driven rapidly along in the post-chaise he said to me, 'Life has not many things better than this.'"—Boswell's *Johnson*, ii. 453.

[2] "He expatiated on the felicity of England in its taverns and inns, and triumphed over the French for not having in any perfection the tavern life. . . . No, sir; there is nothing which has yet been contrived by man by which so much happiness is produced as by a good tavern or inn."—*Ib.*, p. 451.

such as we expect them.   He that has pictured a
prospect upon his fancy, will receive little pleasure
from his eyes ; he that has anticipated the conversation of a wit, will wonder to what prejudice
he owes his reputation.   Yet it is necessary to
hope, though hope should always be deluded ;
for hope itself is happiness, and its frustra-
tions, however frequent, are yet less dreadful
than its extinction.

No. 60. SATURDAY, JUNE 9, 1759.

CRITICISM is a study by which men
grow important and formidable at a
very small expense.   The power of
invention has been conferred by nature
upon few, and the labour of learning those
sciences which may by mere labour be obtained
is too great to be willingly endured ; but every
man can exert such |judgment as he has upon the
works of others ; and he whom nature has made
weak, and idleness keeps ignorant, may yet
support his vanity by the name of a Critic.

I hope it will give comfort to great numbers
who are passing through the world in obscurity,
when I inform them how easily distinction may be
obtained.   All the other powers of literature are
coy and haughty, they must be long courted, and
at last are not always gained ; but Criticism is a
goddess easy of access and forward of advance,
who will meet the slow, and encourage the timorous ; the want of meaning she supplies with

words, and the want of spirit she recompenses with malignity.

This profession has one recommendation peculiar to itself, that it gives vent to malignity without real mischief. No genius was ever blasted by the breath of critics. The poison, which, if confined, would have burst the heart, fumes away in empty hisses, and malice is set at ease with very little danger to merit. The Critic is the only man whose triumph is without another's pain, and whose greatness does not rise upon another's ruin.

To a study at once so easy and so reputable, so malicious and so harmless, it cannot be necessary to invite my readers by a long or laboured exhortation ; it is sufficient, since all would be Critics if they could, to shew by one eminent example that all can be critics if they will.

Dick Minim, after the common course of puerile studies, in which he was no great proficient, was put an apprentice to a brewer, with whom he had lived two years, when his uncle died in the city, and left him a large fortune in the stocks. Dick had for six months before used the company[1] of the lower players, of whom he had learned to scorn a trade, and, being now at liberty to follow his genius, he resolved to be a man of wit and humour. That he might be properly initiated in his new character, he frequented the coffee-houses near the theatres, where he listened very diligently, day after day, to those who talked of language and sentiments, and unities and

[1] Johnson does not in his *Dictionary* give any example of this idiom "*used* the company."

catastrophes, till by slow degrees he began to think that he understood something of the stage, and hoped in time to talk himself.

But he did not trust so much to natural sagacity as wholly to neglect the help of books. When the theatres were shut, he retired to Richmond with a few select writers, whose opinions he impressed upon his memory by unwearied diligence ;[1] and, when he returned with other wits to the town, was able to tell, in very proper phrases, that the chief business of art is to copy nature ;[2] that a perfect writer is not to be expected,[3] because genius decays as judgment increases ;[4] that the great art is the art of blotting ;[5] and that, according to the rule of Horace, every piece should be kept nine years.[6]

[1] In what follows Johnson puts into Minim's mouth opinions gathered from these writers. In the following notes I have traced his course wherever I could; and have shown also in one or two cases Johnson's own opinions subsequently expressed.

[2] "First follow nature, and your judgment frame
By her just standard, which is still the same."
—Pope, *Essay on Criticism*, l. 68.

[3] "Whoever thinks a faultless piece to see,
Thinks what ne'er was, nor is, nor e'er shall be."
—*Ib.*, l. 253.

[4] "Thus in the soul while memory prevails,
The solid power of understanding fails ;
Where beams of warm imagination play,
The memory's soft figures melt away."
—*Ib.*, l. 56.

[5] "Ev'n copious Dryden wanted, or forgot,
The last and greatest art, the art to blot."
—Pope, *Imitations of Horace*, Epis. ii., i. 280.

[6] "And drop at last, but in unwilling ears,
This saving counsel, 'keep your piece nine years.'"

Of the great authors he now began to display the characters, laying down as an universal posi- tion, that all had beauties and defects. His opinion was, that Shakespear, committing himself wholly to the impulse of nature, wanted that cor- rectness which learning would have given him ;[1] and that Jonson, trusting to learning, did not sufficiently cast his eye on nature.[2] He blamed the *stanza* of Spenser, and could not bear the *hexameters* of Sidney.[3] Denham and Waller he held the first reformers of English numbers[4] ; and thought that if Waller could have obtained the strength of Denham, or Denham the sweetness of Waller, there had been nothing wanting to

[1] "——fluent Shakespeare scarce effaced a line."
> —Pope, *Imitations of Horace*, Epis. ii. 1, 279.

" To move, to raise, to ravish every heart,
  With Shakespeare's nature, or with Jonson's art."
> —Pope, *The Dunciad*, ii. 223.

[2] "Too nicely Jonson knew the critic's part ;
  Nature in him was almost lost in art."
> —Collins, *Epistle to Hanmer*, l. 55.

"Then Jonson came, instructed from the school
To please in method, and invent by rule."
> —Johnson's *Prologue at the Opening of Drury
> Lane Theatre, Works*, i. 23.

[3] " Spenser himself affects the obsolete,
  And Sydney's verse halts ill on Roman feet."
> —Pope, *Imitations of Horace*, Epis. ii., i. 97.

[4] " Our numbers were in their nonage till Waller and Den- ham appeared."—Dryden, *Preface to the Fables*. " Denham is deservedly considered as one of the fathers of English poetry. ' Denham and Waller,' says Prior, ' improved our versification, and Dryden perfected it.' "—Johnson's *Works* vii. 60.

complete a poet.[1] He often expressed his commisera
tion of Dryden's poverty, and his indignation at
the age which suffered him to write for bread[2];
he repeated with rapture the first lines of *All for
Love*, but wondered at the corruption of taste
which could bear any thing so unnatural as
rhyming tragedies.[3]   In Otway he found uncommon powers of moving the passions, but was

[1] "And praise the easy vigour of a line,
    Where Denham's strength and Waller's sweetness join."
                    —Pope, *Essay on Criticism*, l. 361.
"The critical decision has given the praise of strength to
Denham, and of sweetness to Waller."—Johnson's *Works*, vii.
215.   Pope, I suspect, borrowed from Dryden, who says:—
"If I should instruct some of my fellow poets to make well-
running verses, they want genius to give them *strength* as
well as *sweetness*."—Dryden's *Works*, ed. 1821, xiv. 204.

[2] Cf. Pope's lines on Dryden's funeral :—
    "But still the great have kindness in reserve,
    He help'd to bury whom he help'd to starve."
                    —*Prologue to the Satires*, l. 247.

[3] *All for Love* is founded upon Shakespeare's *Antony
and Cleopatra*.   Dryden says in the Preface :—"In my
style I have professed to imitate the Divine Shakespeare ;
which that I might perform more freely, I have disencum-
bered myself from rhyme."   The passage which Minim
repeated so rapturously is, I conjecture, the following :—

    "Last night, between the hours of twelve and one,
    In a lone aisle o' th' Temple while I walk'd,
    A whirlwind rose, that with a violent blast
    Shook all the dome: the doors around me clapt,
    The iron wicket that defends the vault
    Where the long race of Ptolemies is laid,
    Burst open, and disclosed the mighty dead.
    From out each monument, in order placed,
    An armed ghost starts up: the Boy-King last
    Reared his inglorious head."

disgusted by his general negligence,[1] and blamed him for making a conspirator his hero[2];¦ and never concluded his disquisition, without remarking how happily the sound of the clock is made to alarm the audience.[3]   Southern would have been his favourite, but that he mixes comic with tragic scenes, intercepts the natural course of the passions, and fills the mind with a wild confusion of mirth and melancholy. The versification of Rowe he thought too melodious for the stage, and too little varied in different passions.[4] He made it the great fault of Congreve, that all his persons were wits, and that he always wrote with more art than nature.[5]   He considered *Cato* rather as a poem than a play,[6] and allowed Addison to be the

[1] "—— Otway failed to polish or refine."
—Pope, *Imitations of Horace, Epis.* ii., i. 278.

[2] "It has been observed by others that this poet has founded his tragedy of *Venice Preserved* on so wrong a plot, that the greatest characters in it are those of rebels and traitors."—*The Spectator*, No 39.

[3] In the last scene but one the passing-bell tolls. Johnson, speaking of Brown's *Barbarossa*, says :—" Otway had tolled a bell before Dr. Brown, and we are not to be made April fools twice by the same trick."—Murphy's *Life of Garrick*, p . 173.

[4] "In a word, Rowe's plays are musical and pleasing poems, but inactive and unmoving tragedies."—J. Warton's *Essay on Pope*, ed. 1762, i. 271.

[5] "His characters are commonly fictitious and artificial, with very little of nature, and not much of life. He formed a peculiar idea of comic excellence. which he supposed to consist in gay remarks and unexpected answers."—Johnson's *Works*, viii. 31.

[6] " *Cato* is a fine dialogue on liberty and the love of one's country."—Warton's *Essay on Pope*, i. 259.

complete master of allegory and grave humour,[1] but paid no great deference to him as a critic.[2] He thought the chief merit of Prior was in his easy tales and lighter poems, though he allowed that his Solomon had many noble sentiments elegantly expressed. In Swift he discovered an inimitable vein of irony, and an easiness which all would hope and few would attain.[3] Pope he was inclined to degrade from a poet to a versifier,[4] and thought his numbers rather luscious than sweet. He often lamented the neglect of Phædra and Hippolitus,[5] and wished to see the stage under better regulations.

[1] "The chief and characteristical excellency of Addison was his humour."—Warton's *Essay on Pope*, p. 269.

[2] "Addison in his life, and for some time afterwards, was considered by the greater part of readers as supremely excelling both in poetry and criticism. . . . A great writer [Warburton] has lately styled him 'an indifferent poet, and a worse critic.'"—Johnson's *Works*, vii. 451.

[3]   "Ut sibi quivis
Speret idem, sudet multum, frustraque laboret,
Ausus idem."—Horace, *Ars Poetica*, l. 240.
Pope in the *Dunciad*, i. 21, addressing Swift, says:—
"Whether thou choose Cervantes' serious air,
Or laugh and shake in Rabelais' easy chair."

[4] The tendency of the first part of Warton's *Essay* was to degrade Pope, if not to a versifier, at all events to a much lower rank than that in which he had been hitherto placed. Johnson referred, I think, to Warton when he wrote:—"After all this it is surely superfluous to answer the question that has once been asked, whether Pope was a poet, otherwise than by asking in return, if Pope be not a poet, where is poetry to be found?"—Johnson's *Works*, viii. 345.

[5] A tragedy by Edmund Smith. Addison, in the *Spectator*, No. 18, writing of its failure, asks:—Would one think it was possible (at a time when an author lived that was able to

These assertions passed commonly uncontra-
dicted ; and if now and then an opponent started
up, he was quickly repressed by the suffrages
of the company, and Minim went away from
every dispute with elation of heart and increase
of confidence.

He now grew conscious of his abilities, and
began to talk of the present state of dramatic
poetry ; wondered what was become of the
comic genius which supplied our ancestors with
wit and pleasantry, and why no writer could be
found that durst now venture beyond a farce.
He saw no reason for thinking that the vein of
humour was exhausted, since we live in a country
where liberty suffers every character to spread
itself to its utmost bulk, and which therefore
produces more originals than all the rest of
the world together.[1] Of tragedy he concluded

---

write the *Phœdra and Hippolitus*) for a people to be so
stupidly fond of the Italian opera, as scarce to give a third
day's hearing to that admirable tragedy ? " Johnson on this
remarks:—"The authority of Addison is great ; yet the
voice of the people, when to please the people is the purpose,
deserves regard. In this question I cannot but think the
people in the right."—Johnson's *Works*, vii. 376.

1 Minim, I suspect, is borrowing from Johnson's *Preface to
the Harleian Miscellany*, where he writes :—" It is observed
that among the natives of England is to be found a greater
variety of humour than in any other country ; and, doubtless,
where every man has a full liberty to propagate his conceptions, variety of humour must produce variety of writers,
and where the number of authors is so great, there cannot
but be some worthy of distinction."—Johnson's *Works*, v.
192. Johnson refers most likely to Temple's Essay *Of
Poetry.*—Temple's *Works,* ed. 1757, iii. 425.

business to be the soul, and yet often hinted that love predominates too much upon the modern stage.

He was now an acknowledged critic, and had his own seat in a coffee-house, and headed a party in the pit. Minim has more vanity than ill-nature, and seldom desires to do much mischief ; he will perhaps murmur a little in the ear of him that sits next him, but endeavours to influence the audience to favour, by clapping when an actor exclaims *ye gods*, or laments the misery of his country.

By degrees he was admitted to rehearsals, and many of his friends are of opinion, that our present poets are indebted to him, for their happiest thoughts ; by his contrivance the bell was rung twice in *Barbarossa*, and by his persuasion the author of *Cleone*[1] concluded his play without a couplet ; for what can be more absurd, said Minim, than that part of a play should be rhymed, and part written in blank verse ? and by what acquisition of faculties is the speaker, who never could find rhymes before, enabled to rhyme at the conclusion of an act ?[2]

He is the great investigator of hidden beauties, and is particularly delighted when he finds *the*

[1] By Robert Dodsley. It was of this play that Johnson said, when Bennet Langton had read aloud to him an act :— " Come, let's have some more, let's go into the slaughter-house again, Lanky. But I am afraid there is more blood than brains."—Boswell's *Johnson*, iv. 20.

[2] Johnson, in accordance with what was, if not the invariable, at all events the almost invariable practice, concluded every act of his *Irene* with a rhyme.

sound an echo to the sense.[1] He has read all our poets with particular attention to this delicacy of versification, and wonders at the supineness with which their works have been hitherto perused, so that no man has found the sound of a drum in this distich ;

> " When pulpit, drum ecclesiastic,
> Was beat with fist instead of a stick ;"[2]

and that the wonderful lines upon honour and a bubble have hitherto passed without notice :

> " Honour is like the glassy bubble,
> Which cost philosophers such trouble ;
> Where, one part crack'd, the whole does fly,
> And wits are crack'd to find out why."[3]

In these verses, says Minim, we have two striking accommodations of the sound to the sense.[4] It is impossible to utter the two lines emphatically without an act like that which they describe ; *bubble* and *trouble* causing a momentary inflation of the cheeks by the retention of the breath which is afterwards forcibly emitted, as in the practice of *blowing bubbles.* But the greatest

[1] " 'Tis not enough no harshness gives offence,
The sound must seem an echo to the sense."
Pope, *Essay on Criticism,* 1. 364.

[2] *Hudibras,* i. 1, 11.

[3] " Honour is like that glassy bubble
That finds philosophers such trouble,
Whose least part crack'd the whole does fly,
And wits are crack'd to find out why."
—*Ib.,* ii. 2, 385.

[4] Minim here quotes the *Rambler,* No. 92 :—"There is nothing in the art of versifying so much exposed to the power of imagination as the accommodation of the sound to the sense."

excellence is in the third line, which is *crack'd* in the middle to express a crack, and then shivers into monosyllables. Yet has this diamond laid neglected with common stones, and among the innumerable admirers of *Hudibras* the observation of this superlative passage has been reserved for the sagacity of Minim.

No. 61. SATURDAY, JUNE 15, 1759.

MR. MINIM had now advanced himself to the zenith of critical reputation ; when he was in the pit, every eye in the boxes was fixed upon him ; when he entered his coffee-house, he was surrounded by circles of candidates, who passed their novitiate of literature under his tuition : his opinion was asked by all who had no opinion of their own, and yet loved to debate and decide ; and no composition was supposed to pass in safety to posterity, till it had been secured by Minim's approbation.

Minim professes great admiration of the wisdom and munificence by which the academies of the Continent were raised ; and often wishes for some standard of taste, for some tribunal, to which merit may appeal from caprice, prejudice, and malignity. He has formed a plan for an academy of criticism, where every work of imagination may be read before it is printed, and which shall authoritatively direct the theatres what pieces to receive or reject, to exclude or to revive.[1]

Such an institution would, in *Dick's* opinion spread the fame of English literature over *Europe*, and make London the metropolis of elegance and politeness, the place to which the learned and ingenious of all countries would repair for instruction and improvement, where nothing would any longer be applauded or endured that was not conformed to the nicest rules, and finished with the highest elegance.

Till some happy conjunction of the planets shall dispose our princes or ministers to make themselves immortal by such an academy, Minim contents himself to preside four nights in a week in a critical society selected by himself, where he is heard without contradiction, and whence his judgment is disseminated through the great vulgar and the small.[2]

When he is placed in the chair of criticism, he declares loudly for the noble simplicity of our ancestors, in opposition to the petty refinements, and ornamental luxuriance. Sometimes he is sunk in despair, and perceives false delicacy daily gaining ground, and sometimes brightens his countenance with a gleam of hope, and predicts the revival of the true sublime. He then

[1] So Roscommon, Prior, Swift, and Tickell had each planned a Society or an Academy for "refining our language and fixing its standard."—Johnson's *Works*, v. 49 ; vii. 167 ; viii. 4, 202.

[2] " Hence ye prophane ; I hate ye all,
Both the Great Vulgar, and the Small."
—Cowley, *Imitations of Horace*, Odes iii. 1.

fulminates his loudest censures against the monkish barbarity of rhyme[1] ; wonders how beings that pretend to reason can be pleased with one line always ending like another ; tells how unjustly and unnaturally sense is sacrificed to sound ; how often the best thoughts are mangled by the necessity of confining or extending them to the dimensions of a couplet ; and rejoices that genius has, in our days, shaken off the shackles which had encumbered it so long.[2] Yet he allows that rhyme may sometimes be borne, if the lines be often broken, and the pauses judiciously diversified.

[1] " Rhyme is the invention of a barbarous age to set off wretched matter and lame metre ; graced indeed since by the use of some famous modern poets, carried away by custom, but much to their own vexation, hindrance and constraint, to express many things otherwise, and for the most part worse than else they would have expressed them."— Preface to *Paradise Lost.*

" Rise, rise, Roscommon, see the Blenheim muse
The dull constraint of monkish rhyme refuse."
—Edmund Smith, quoted in Johnson's *Dictionary.*

Dryden says that " Hannibal Caro freed himself from the shackles of modern rhyme....What rhyme adds to sweetness, it takes away from sense."—Dryden's *Works,* ed. 1821, xiv. 206. Warton, in his *Essay on Pope,* i. 192, speaks of " daring to throw off the bondage of rhyme."

[2] Goldsmith, writing in this same year, 1759, differed from the great Minim. " From a desire in the critic of grafting the spirit of ancient languages upon the English have proceeded of late several disagreeable instances of pedantry. Among the number, I think, we may reckon blank verse. . . . We now see it used upon the most trivial occasions."—*Present State of Polite Learning,* ch. xi. Among the poets who had lately written in blank verse were *Thomson,* Watts, Dyer, Shenstone, Young, Akenside, and Lyttelton.

From blank verse he makes an easy transition
to Milton, whom he produces as an example of
the slow advance of lasting reputation. Milton is
the only writer in whose books Minim can read
for ever without weariness.[1] What cause it is that
exempts this pleasure from satiety he has long
and diligently inquired, and believes it to consist
in the perpetual variation of the numbers, by
which the ear is gratified and the attention
awakened.[2] The lines that are commonly thought
rugged and unmusical, he conceives to have been
written to temper the melodious luxury of the
rest, or to express things by a proper cadence :
for he scarcely finds a verse that has not this
favourite beauty ; he declares that he could shiver
in a hot-house when he reads that

" the ground
" Burns frore, and cold performs th' effect of fire[3] ;

and that, when Milton bewails his blindness, the
verse,

" So thick a drop serene has quench'd these orbs,"[4]

has, he knows not how, something that strikes
him with an obscure sensation like that which he
fancies would be felt from the sound of darkness.

---

[1] Johnson differed from Minim in this. " None ever wished
Paradise Lost longer than it is. Its perusal is a duty
rather than a pleasure."—Johnson's *Works*, vii. 135.

[2] Perhaps borrowed from *The Rambler*, No. 86. See
ante vol. i., p. 169.

[3]   " The *parching air*,
    Burns frore," etc.—*Paradise Lost*, ii. 594.

[4] " So thick a drop serene hath quenched *their* orbs."
Ib., iii. 25.
Johnson did not " verify his quotations."

Minim is not so confident of his rules of judgment as not very eagerly to catch new light from the name of the author. He is commonly so prudent as to spare those whom he cannot resist, unless, as will sometimes happen, he finds the public combined against them. But a fresh pretender to fame he is strongly inclined to censure, till his own honour requires that he commend him. Till he knows the success of a composition, he intrenches himself in general terms; there are some new thoughts and beautiful passages, but there is likewise much which he would have advised the author to expunge. He has several favourite epithets, of which he has never settled the meaning, but which are very commodiously applied to books which he has not read, or cannot understand. One is *manly*, another is *dry*, another *stiff*, and another *flimsy*[1]; sometimes he discovers delicacy of style, and sometimes meets with *strange expressions*.

He is never so great, or so happy, as when a youth of promising parts is brought to receive his directions for the prosecution of his studies. He then puts on a very serious air; he advises the pupil to read none but the best authors, and, when he finds one congenial to his own mind, to study his beauties, but avoid his faults; and, when he sits down to write, to consider how his favourite author would think at the present time on the present occasion. He exhorts him to catch those moments when he finds his thoughts expanded

[1] "Proud of a vast extent of flimsy lines."

Pope, *Prologue to the Satires*, l. 96.

and his genius exalted, but to take care lest imagination hurry him beyond the bounds of nature. He holds diligence the mother of success ; yet enjoins him, with great earnestness, not to read more than he can digest, and not to confuse his mind by pursuing studies of contrary tenden-cies. He tells him, that every man has his genius,[1] and that Cicero could never be a poet. The boy retires illuminated, resolves to follow his genius,[2] and to think how Milton would have thought : and Minim feasts upon his own bene-ficence till another day brings another pupil.

No. 65. SATURDAY, JULY 14, 1759.

THE sequel of Clarendon's history, at last happily published, is an accession to English literature equally agreeable to the admirers of elegance and the lovers of truth ; many doubtful facts may now be ascertained, and many questions, after long debate, may be determined by decisive authority. He that records transactions in which himself was engaged, has not only an opportunity of knowing innumerable particulars which escape spectators, but has his natural powers exalted by that ardour which always rises at the remembrance of our own

1 Johnson always maintained the opposite of this. "The true genius," he says in the beginning of his *Life of Cowley*, "is a mind of large general powers, accidentally determined to some particular direction."

2 "The general precept of consulting the genius is of little use, unless we are told how the genius can be known."—*Rambler* No. 19.

importance, and by which every man is enabled
to relate his own actions better than another's.

The difficulties through which this work has
struggled into light, and the delays with which
our hopes have been long mocked,[1] naturally lead
the mind to the consideration of the common fate
of posthumous compositions.

He who sees himself surrounded by admirers,
and whose vanity is hourly feasted with all the
luxuries of studied praise, is easily persuaded that
his influence will be extended beyond his life ;
that they who cringe in his presence will reverence
his memory, and that those who are proud to be
numbered among his friends, will endeavour to
vindicate his choice by zeal for his reputation.

[1] Lord Hyde, the heir to the Earldom of Clarendon, had
left by his will this work, "and the other remains of his
great-grandfather, in the hands of trustees, to be printed at
the Clarendon Press, and directed that the profits arising
from the sale should be employed towards the establishing a
riding-school in the University. But dying before his father
[they both died in 1753], the property of these papers never
became vested in him, and consequently this bequest was
void." The heiresses of the Earl fulfilled Lord Hyde's intention, and left them to the University " on condition that the
profits be applied as a beginning for a fund for supporting a
Manage, or Academy for Riding, and other useful exercises
in Oxford."—*Life of the Earl of Clarendon*, ed. 1759, Preface. Johnson took much interest in this scheme, but nothing
came of it.—Boswell's *Johnson*, ii. 424. "On Feb. 4, 1868,
a scheme for the appropriation of the accumulated fund (now
amounting to about £12,000) which had been approved by
the Clarendon trustees was accepted by Convocation. The
money is to be applied to the erection of laboratories, etc.,
at the University Museum." Macray's *Annals of the
Bodleian*, p. 163. The Clarendon Laboratory indicates its
origin by its name.

With hopes like these, to the executors of Swift was committed the history of the last years of Queen Anne,[1] and to those of Pope, the works which remained unprinted in his closet. The performances of Pope were burnt by those whom he had perhaps selected from all mankind as most likely to publish them[2]; and the history had likewise perished, had not a straggling transcript fallen into busy hands.[3]

The papers left in the closet of Peiresc supplied his heirs with a whole winter's fuel[4]; and many of

[1] This work had been published the year before. Johnson, in his *Life of Swift*, doubts its genuineness (Johnson's *Works*, viii. 207); but, it should seem, without reason.—See Craik's *Life of Swift*, ed. 1882, p. 518.

[2] "Pope left the care of his papers to his executors. . . . undoubtedly expecting them to be proud of the trust, and eager to extend his fame. But let no man dream of influence beyond his life. After a decent time Dodsley, the bookseller, went to solicit preference as the publisher, and was told that the parcel had not been yet inspected; and whatever was the reason, the world has been disappointed of what was 'reserved for the next age.'"—Johnson's *Works*, viii. 306.

[3] According to the Advertisement prefixed to Swift's *History*, a manuscript copy, which he had lent to a friend, had never been reclaimed. When this man learnt that the Dean's executors "had suppressed, perhaps destroyed the original copy," he printed the one which he had.

[4] "A chamber in his house was filled with letters from the most eminent scholars of the age. The learned in Europe had addressed Peiresc in their difficulties, who was hence called the *avocat-général* of the republic of letters." His niggardly niece, though entreated to permit them to be published, preferred to use these learned epistles occasionally to light her fires.—D'Israeli's *Curiosities of Literature*, ed. 1834, i. 78. "Peiresc's death (said Johnson) was lamented, I think, in forty languages."—Boswell's *Johnson*, ii. 371.

the labours of the learned Bishop Lloyd were consumed in the kitchen of his descendants.[1]

Some works, indeed, have escaped total destruction, but yet have had reason to lament the fate of orphans exposed to the frauds of unfaithful guardians. How Hale would have borne the mutilations which his *Pleas of the Crown* have suffered from the editor, they who know his character will easily conceive.[2]

The original copy of Burnet's history, though promised to some public library,[3] has been never

[1] " He (Lloyd) had read the most books, and had made the most copious abstracts out of them, of any in this age ; so that Wilkins used to say, he had the most learning in ready cash of any he ever knew."—Burnet's *History of his own Times*, ed. 1818, i. 210. He was one of the Seven Bishops sent to the Tower in 1688 ; but the kitchen of his descendants perhaps did no great mischief, if Macaulay's statement is true, that he was "half crazed by his persevering endeavours to extract from the Book of Daniel and from the Revelations some information about the Pope and the King of France."—*History of England*, ed. 1873, iii. 84.

[2] Burnet, at the end of his *Life of Hale*, says that "the reason that made that Judge so unwilling to have any of his works printed after his death was, that he apprehended in the licensing them some things might have been struck out or altered. This in matters of law, he said, might prove to be of such mischievous consequences that he thereupon resolved none of his writings should be at the mercy of licensers."

[3] It would be proper to reposit, in some public place, the manuscript of *Clarendon*, which has not escaped all suspicion of unfaithful publication.—*Johnson.* The manuscript is in the Bodleian Library, having been deposited there, as it seems, in 1759.—Macray's *Annals*, p. 163. From it Mr. Bandinel printed the Oxford edition of 1826. He states, in the Preface, that though the first editors sometimes softened certain parts, or omitted " an unfavourable

given[1]; and who then can prove the fidelity of the publication, when the authenticity of Clarendon's history, though printed with the sanction of one of the first universities in the world, had not an unexpected manuscript been happily discovered, would, with the help of factious credulity, have been brought into question by the two lowest of all human beings, a scribbler for a party, and a commissioner of excise. [2]

---

part of a character not absolutely necessary to illustrate any particular transaction, they in no one instance added, suppressed, or altered any historical fact." A perfect, and therefore a final collation, of the text has been made by the Rev. W. D. Macray for his edition printed last year at the Clarendon Press.

[1] The original MS. or "copy" of Burnet's *History of his Own Times* was purchased, with some other papers, for the Bodleian Library in 1835 for £210.—Macray's *Annals of the Bodleian*, p. 252.

[2] "The persons to whom Johnson alludes (writes Boswell) were Mr. John Oldmixon and George Duckett, Esq."—Boswell's *Johnson*, i. 295. "Duckett informed Oldmixon that Clarendon's *History* was before publication corrupted by Aldrich, Smalridge, and Atterbury, and that Edmund Smith before he died confessed to having helped them, and pointed out some spurious passages. A bitter controversy resulted; Duckett's charge entirely broke down, and it is now unknown who was primarily responsible. Duckett was one of the commissioners of excise from 1722 to 1732."—*Dict. of Nat. Biog.*, xvi. 91. In the "advertisement" to the Oxford edition of Clarendon's *History* of 1732, it is stated:—" Tho' the improbable story handed into the world by one Oldmixon deserves no farther notice, yet to prevent any person's being imposed upon by so gross and bold a fiction, there is part of the Life of the Lord Chancellor Clarendon, written ALL in his Lordship's OWN HAND, lodged in the Bodleian Library, to remain there for twelve months." This part contained

Vanity is often no less mischievous than negligence or dishonesty. He that possesses a valuable manuscript, hopes to raise its esteem by concealment, and delights in the distinction which he imagines himself to obtain, by keeping the key of a treasure which he neither uses nor imparts. From him it falls to some other owner, less vain but more negligent, who considers it as useless lumber, and rids himself of the incumbrance.

Yet there are some works which the authors must consign unpublished to posterity, however uncertain be the event, however hopeless be the trust. He that writes the history of his own times, if he adheres steadily to truth, will write that which his own times will not easily endure. He must be content to reposite his book till all private passions shall cease, and love and hatred give way to curiosity.

But many leave the labours of half their life to their executors and to chance, because they will not send them abroad unfinished, and are unable to finish them, having prescribed to themselves such a degree of exactness as human diligence can scarcely attain. Lloyd, says Burnet, *did not lay out his learning with the same diligence as he laid it*

---

one of the passages which Oldmixon had asserted was not in the original. Johnson had defined *excise* as *a hateful tax levied upon commodities, and adjudged not by the common judges of property, but by wretches hired by those to whom excise is paid.* In the *Rambler*, No. 12, he makes the wife of a Commissioner of Excise a very brutal woman.

in.[1] He was always hesitating and inquiring raising objections and removing them, and waiting for clearer light and fuller discovery. Baker,[2] after many years passed in biography, left his manuscripts to be buried in a library, because that was imperfect, which could never be perfected.

Of these learned men, let those who aspire to the same praise, imitate the diligence, and avoid the scrupulosity.[3] Let it be always remembered that life is short, that knowledge is endless, and that many doubts deserve not to be cleared. Let those whom nature and study have qualified to teach mankind, tell us what they have learned while they are yet able to tell it, and trust their reputation only to themselves.

[1] "He was so exact in everything he set about that he never gave over any part of study till he had quite mastered it ; but when that was done he went to another subject, and did not lay out his learning with the diligence with which he laid it in."—Burnet's *History*, i. 210.

[2] Thomas Baker, the author and antiquary (1656—1740). "At his death the greater part of his collections came into the possession of the College [St John's, Cambridge], and the shelves of the library were enlarged for their reception." —*Dict. of Nat. Biog.*, iii. 20.

[3] *Scrupulosity* was a favourite word with Johnson. Sir William Jones, writing in 1776, said :—"You will be able to examine with the minutest *scrupulosity*, as Johnson would call it."—*Life of Sir William Jones*, p. 177.

No. 74. SATURDAY, SEPTEMBER 15, 1759.

IN the mythological pedigree of learning, memory is made the mother of the muses, by which the masters of ancient wisdom, perhaps, meant to shew the necessity of storing the mind copiously with true notions, before the imagination should be suffered to form fictions or collect embellishments ;[1] for the works of an ignorant poet can afford nothing higher than pleasing sound, and fiction is of no other use than to display the treasures of memory.

The necessity of memory to the acquisition of knowledge is inevitably felt and universally allowed, so that scarcely any other of the mental faculties are commonly considered as necessary to a student : he that admires the proficiency of another, always attributes it to the happiness of his memory ; and he that laments his own defects concludes with a wish that his memory was better.

It is evident, that when the power of retention is weak, all the attempts at eminence of knowledge must be vain ; and as few are willing to be doomed to perpetual ignorance, I may, perhaps, afford consolation to some that have fallen too easily into despondence, by observing that such

[1] Before the invention of writing memory was the poet's excellence ; therefore Mnemosyne was called the mother of the Muses.—See Liddell and Scott's *Greek Lexicon*.

weakness is, in my opinion, very rare, and that few have reason to complain of nature as unkindly sparing of the gifts of memory.[1]

In the common business of life, we find the memory of one like that of another, and honestly impute omissions not to involuntary forgetfulness, but culpable inattention ; but in literary inquiries, failure is imputed rather to want of memory than of diligence.

We consider ourselves as defective in memory, either because we remember less than we desire, or less than we suppose others to remember.

Memory is like all other human powers, with which no man can be satisfied who measures them by what he can conceive, or by what he can desire. He whose mind is most capacious, finds it much too narrow for his wishes : he that remembers most, remembers little compared with what he forgets. He therefore that, after the perusal of a book, finds few ideas remaining in his mind, is not to consider the disappointment as peculiar to himself, or to resign all hopes of improvement, because, he does not retain what even the author has perhaps forgotten.

He who compares his memory with that of others, is often too hasty to lament the inequality. Nature has sometimes, indeed, afforded examples of enormous, wonderful, and gigantic memory. Scaliger reports of himself, that, in his youth, he could repeat above an hundred verses, having

---

[1] Boswell mentions that Johnson one day "maintained that forgetfulness was a man's own fault."—Boswell's *John-son*, iv. 126.

once read them[1] ; and Barthius[2] declares that he
wrote his *comment upon Claudian* without consulting the text.[3]   But not to have such degrees
of memory, is no more to be lamented, than not to
have the strength of Hercules, or the swiftness of
Achilles.   He that, in the distribution of good,
has an equal share with common men, may justly
be contented.   Where there is no striking dis-
parity, it is difficult to know of two which remembers most, and still more difficult to discover
which reads with greater attention, which has
renewed the first impression by more frequent
repetitions, or by what accidental combination of
ideas either mind might have united any particular narrative or argument to its former stock.

[1] Boswell records the following instance of Johnson's
powerful memory :—"We had this morning a singular
proof of Dr. Johnson's quick and retentive memory. Hay's
translation of *Martial* was lying in a window ; I said, I
thought it was pretty well done, and showed him a particular epigram, I think, of ten, but am certain, of eight lines.
He read it, and tossed away the book, saying, ' No, it is *not*
pretty well.'   As I persisted in my opinion, he said, ' Why
sir, the original is thus,' and he repeated it, 'and this man's
translation is thus' ; and then he repeated that also exactly,
though he had never seen it before, and read it over only
once, and that too without any intention of getting it by
heart."—Boswell's *Johnson*, v. 368.

[2] Gaspar Barthius published his *Comment* in 1650. In
most of the editions of the *Idler*, even of those published in
Johnson's life-time, the name is printed *Barthicus*.

[3] "*The Life of Rowe* (says Nichols) is a very remarkable
instance of the uncommon strength of Dr. Johnson's memory.
When I received from him the MS. he complacently observed that the criticism was tolerably well done, considering
that he had not read one of Rowe's plays for thirty years."—
Boswell's *Johnson*, iv. 36.

But memory, however impartially distributed, so often deceives our trust, that almost every man attempts, by some artifice or other, to secure its fidelity.

It is the practice of many readers to note, in the margin of their books, the most important passages, the strongest arguments, or the brightest sentiments. Thus they load their minds with superfluous attention, repress the vehemence of curiosity by useless deliberation, and by frequent interruption break the current of narration or the chain of reason, and at last close the volume, and forget the passages and marks together.

Others I have found unalterably persuaded, that nothing is certainly remembered but what is transcribed; and they have therefore passed weeks and months in transferring large quotations to a common-place book. Yet, why any part of a book, which can be consulted at pleasure, should be copied, I was never able to discover. The hand has no closer correspondence with the memory than the eye. The act of writing itself distracts the thoughts, and what is read twice is commonly better remembered than what is transcribed.[1]

---

[1] Gibbon, describing his studies, says:—"This various reading was digested, according to the precept and model of Mr. Locke, into a large common-place book; a practice, however, which I do not strenuously recommend. The action of the pen will doubtless imprint an idea on the mind as well as on the paper; but I much question whether the benefits of this laborious method are adequate to the waste of time, and I must agree with Dr. Johnson that 'what is twice read is commonly better remembered than what is transcribed.'" —Gibbon's *Misc. Works,* i. 97.

This method therefore consumes time without assisting memory.

The true art of memory is the art of attention. No man will read with much advantage, who is not able, at pleasure to evacuate his mind, or who brings not to his author an intellect defecated and pure, neither turbid with care, nor agitated by pleasure.[1] If the repositories of thought are already full, what can they receive?[2] If the mind is employed on the past or future, the book will be held before the eyes in vain. What is read with delight is commonly retained, because pleasure always secures attention[3]; but the books which are consulted by occasional necessity, and perused with impatience, seldom leave any traces on the mind.

[1] We have here striking instances of Johnson's style at its best and worst. Nothing could be better said than that "the true art of memory is the art of attention." What follows is the worst kind of *Johnsonese.*

[2] "Omne supervacuum pleno de pectore manat."
—*Ars Poetica*, l. 337.

[3] "No profit grows where is no pleasure ta'en ;
In brief, sir, study what you most affect."
—*The Taming of the Shrew*, act i., sc. 1., l. 39.

"A man (said Johnson) ought to read just as inclination leads him ; for what he reads as a task will do him little good."—Boswell's *Johnson*, i. 428. "What we read with inclination makes a much stronger impression. If we read without inclination, half the mind is employed in fixing the attention ; so there is but one half to be employed on what we read."—*Ib.*, iii. 43.

No. 78. SATURDAY, OCTOBER 13, 1759.

HAVE passed the summer in one of those places to which a mineral spring gives the idle and luxurious an annual reason for resorting, whenever they fancy themselves offended by the heat of London. What is the true motive of this periodical assembly, I have never yet been able to discover. The greater part of the visitants neither feel diseases nor fear them. What pleasure can be expected more than the variety of the journey, I know not, for the numbers are too great for privacy, and too small for diversion. As each is known to be a spy upon the rest, they all live in continual restraint ; and having but a narrow range for censure, they gratify its cravings by preying on one another.

But every condition has some advantages. In this confinement, a smaller circle affords opportunities for more exact observation. The glass that magnifies its object contracts the sight to a point ; and the mind must be fixed upon a single character to remark its minute peculiarities. The quality or habit which passes unobserved in the tumult of successive multitudes, becomes conspicuous when it is offered to the notice day after day ; and perhaps I have, without any distinct notice, seen thousands like my late companions ; for when the scene can be varied at pleasure, a slight disgust

turns us aside before a deep impression can be
made upon the mind.

There was a select set, supposed to be distinguished by superiority of intellects,[1] who always
passed the evening together.   To be admitted to
their conversation was the highest honour of the
place; many youths aspired to distinction, by
pretending to occasional invitations; and the
ladies were often wishing to be men, that they
might partake the pleasures of learned society.

I know not whether by merit or destiny, I
was, soon after my arrival, admitted to this envied
party, which I frequented till I had learned the
art by which each endeavoured to support his
character.

Tom Steady was a vehement assertor of uncon-
troverted truth; and by keeping himself out of
the reach of contradiction, had acquired all the
confidence which the consciousness of irresistible
abilities could have given. I was once mentioning
a man of eminence, and, after having recounted
his virtues, endeavoured to represent him fully,
by mentioning his faults. " Sir," said Mr. Steady,
" that he has faults I can easily believe, for who is
" without them? No man, Sir, is now alive, among
" the innumerable multitudes that swarm upon
" the earth, however wise, or however good, who
" has not, in some degree, his failings and his faults.

1 " One whose *intellects* were exhausted."—*Rasselas*, ch.
iii.   "There is a wicked inclination in most people (said
Johnson) to suppose an old man decayed in his *intellects*."
—Boswell's *Johnson*, iv. 181.   There is no example in
Johnson's *Dictionary* of this use of *intellect* in the
plural.

"If there be any man faultless, bring him forth
"into public view, show him openly, and let him be
"known : but I will venture to affirm, and, till the
"contrary be plainly shown, shall always maintain,
"that no such man is to be found. Tell not me,
"Sir, of impeccability and perfection ; such talk is
"for those that are strangers in the world : I have
"seen several nations, and conversed with all ranks
"of people : I have known the great and the mean,
"the learned and the ignorant, the old and the
"young, the clerical and the lay ; but I have never
"found a man without a fault ; and I suppose
"shall die in the opinion that to be human is to
"be frail."

To all this nothing could be opposed. I listened with a hanging head ; Mr. Steady looked
round on the hearers with triumph, and saw every
eye congratulating his victory ; he departed, and
spent the next morning in following those who
retired from the company, and telling them, with
injunctions of secrecy, how poor Spritely began to
take liberties with men wiser than himself ; but
that he suppressed him by a decisive argument,
which put him totally to silence.

Dick Snug is a man of sly remark and pithy
sententiousness : he never immerges himself in
the stream of conversation, but lies to catch his
companions in the eddy, he is often very successful in breaking narratives and confounding
eloquence. A gentleman, giving the history of
one of his acquaintance, made mention of a lady
that had many lovers : "Then," said Dick, "she
"was either handsome or rich." This observation

being well received, Dick watched the progress of
the tale ; and hearing of a man lost in a shipwreck,
remarked, that " no man was every drowned upon
dry land."

Will Startle is a man of exquisite sensibility,
whose delicacy of frame and quickness of dis-
cernment, subject him to impressions from the
slightest causes ; and who therefore passes his
life between rapture and horror, in quiverings
of delight, or convulsions of disgust. His emotions
are too violent for many words ; his thoughts are
always discovered by acclamations. *Vile, odious,
horrid, detestable*, and *sweet, charming, delightful,
astonishing*, compose almost his whole vocabulary,
which he utters with various contortions and ges-
ticulations, not easily related or described.

Jack Solid is a man of much reading, who utters
nothing but quotations ; but having been, I suppose, too confident of his memory, he has for
some time neglected his books, and his stock
grows every day more scanty. Mr. Solid has
found an opportunity every night to repeat, from
Hudibras,

> Doubtless the pleasure is as great
> Of being cheated, as to cheat ; [1]

and from Waller,

> Poets lose half the praise they would have got,
> Were it but known that they discreetly blot.[2]

Dick Misty is a man of deep research, and

[1] *Hudibras,* ii. 3. 1.
[2]   " Poets lose half the praise they should have got,
      Could it be known what they discreetly blot."
—*Upon Roscommon's Translation of Horace, De Arte
Poetica.*

forcible penetration. Others are content with super-
ficial appearances ; but Dick holds, that there is
no effect without a cause, and values himself upon
his power of explaining the difficult, and display-
ing the abstruse. Upon a dispute among us,
which of two young strangers was more beautiful,
" You," says Mr. Misty, turning to me, " like
"Amaranthia better than Chloris. I do not
"wonder at the preference, for the cause is
" evident : there is in man a preception of har-
" mony, and a sensibility of perfection, which
" touches the finer fibres of the mental texture ;
" and before reason can descend from her throne,
" to pass her sentence upon the things compared,
" drives us towards the object proportioned to
" our faculties, by an impulse gentle, yet
" irresistible ; for the harmonic system of the
" Universe, and the reciprocal magnetism of
" similar natures, are always operating towards
" conformity and union ; nor can the powers of
" the soul cease from agitation, till they find some-
"thing on which they can repose." To this
nothing was opposed ; and Amaranthia was
acknowledged to excel Chloris.

Of the rest you may expect an account from,

Sir, yours,

ROBIN SPRITELY.

No. 81. SATURDAY, NOVEMBER 3, 1759.

S the English army was passing towards Quebec along a soft savanna between a mountain and a lake, one of the petty chiefs of the inland region stood upon a rock surrounded by his clan, and from behind the shelter of the bushes contemplated the art and regularity of European war. It was evening, the tents were pitched : he observed the security with which the troops rested in the night, and the order with which the march was renewed in the morning. He continued to pursue them with his eye till they could be seen no longer, and then stood for some time silent and pensive.

Then turning to his followers, "My children " (said he), I have often heard from men hoary " with long life, that there was a time when our " ancestors were absolute lords of the woods, " the meadows, and the lakes, wherever the eye " can reach or the foot can pass. They fished and " hunted, feasted and danced, and when they " were weary lay down under the first thicket, " without danger, and without fear. They " changed their habitations as the seasons re- " quired, convenience prompted, or curiosity al- " lured them ; and sometimes gathered the fruits " of the mountain, and sometimes sported in " canoes along the coast.

" Many years and ages are supposed to have
" been thus passed in plenty and security ; when,
" at last, a new race of men entered our country
" from the great ocean. They inclosed themselves
" in habitations of stone, which our ancestors
" could neither enter by violence, nor destroy by
" fire. They issued from those fastnesses some-
" times covered like the armadillo[1] with shells
" from which the lance rebounded on the striker,
" and sometimes carried by mighty beasts which
" had never been seen in our vales or forests,
" of such strength and swiftness, that flight
" and opposition were vain alike. Those invaders
" ranged over the continent, slaughtering in their
" rage those that resisted, and those that sub-
" mitted, in their mirth. Of those that remained
" some were buried in caverns, and condemned to
" dig metals for their masters ; some were em-
" ployed in tilling the ground, of which foreign
" tyrants devour the produce ; and, when the
" sword and the mines have destroyed the natives,
" they supply their place by human beings of
" another colour, brought from some distant
" country to perish here under toil and torture.

" Some there are who boast their humanity,
" and content themselves to seize our chaces and
" fisheries, who drive us from every track of
" ground where fertility and pleasantness invite
" them to settle, and make no war upon us
" except when we intrude upon our own lands.

" Others pretend to have purchased a right of

1 The armadillo is found in the tropical and temperate
regions of South America, not in Canada.

" residence and tyranny ; but surely the insolence
" of such bargains is more offensive than the
" avowed and open dominion of force. What re-
" ward can induce the possessor of a country to
" admit a stranger more powerful than himself ?
" Fraud or terror must operate in such contracts ;
" either they promised protection which they never
" have afforded, or instruction which they never
" imparted.[1] We hope to be secured by their
" favour from some other evil, or to learn the arts
" of Europe, by which we might be able to secure
" ourselves. Their power they never have exerted
" in our defence, and their arts they have studi-
" ously concealed from us. Their treaties are
" only to deceive, and their traffick only to defraud
" us. They have a written law among them, of
" which they boast as derived from Him who
" made the earth and sea, and by which they pro-
" fess to believe that man will be made happy
" when life shall forsake him. Why is not this law
" communicated to us ?[2] It is concealed because it

[1] Johnson in his *Observations on the State of Affairs in
1756*, had said:—"Some colonies indeed have been established more peaceably than others. The utmost extremity
of wrong has not always been practised ; but those that have
settled in the new world on the fairest terms have no other
merit than that of a scrivener who ruins in silence over a
plunderer that seizes by force."—Johnson's *Works*, vi. 115.

[2] "To omit for a year, or for a day, the most efficacious
method of advancing Christianity, in compliance with any
purposes that terminate on this side of the grave, is a crime
of which I know not that the world has yet had an example,
except in the practice of the planters of America—a race of
mortals whom, I suppose, no other man wishes to resemble."
—Boswell's *Johnson*, ii. 27.

" is violated. For how can they preach it to an
" Indian nation, when I am told that one of its
" first precepts forbids them to do to others
" what they would not that others should do
" to them ?

" But the time perhaps is now approaching
" when the pride of usurpation shall be crushed,
" and the cruelties of invasion shall be revenged.
" The sons of rapacity have now drawn their
" swords upon each other, and referred their
" claims to the decision of war[1] ; let us look un-
" concerned upon the slaughter, and remember
" that the death of every European delivers the
" country from a tyrant and a robber[2] ; for what is
" the claim of either nation, but the claim of the
" vulture to the leveret, of the tiger to the fawn ?
" Let them then continue to dispute their title to
" regions which they cannot people, to purchase
" by danger and blood the empty dignity of do-
" minion over mountains which they will never
" climb, and rivers which they will never pass.
" Let us endeavour, in the mean time, to learn
" their discipline, and to forge their weapons ;
" and, when they shall be weakened with mutual
" slaughter, let us rush down upon them,

1 Johnson, writing of the war between the English and the
French in America, had said :—" Such is the contest that no
honest man can heartily wish success to either party. . . .
The American dispute between the French and us is only
the quarrel of two robbers for the spoils of a passenger."—
Johnson's *Works*, vi. 114, 5.

2   " Tyrants fall in every foe."
                        —Burns, *Scots wha hae*, etc.

" force their remains[1] to take shelter in their
" ships, and reign once more in our native
country."[2]

No. 83. SATURDAY, NOVEMBER 17, 1759.

To the IDLER.

SIR,

SUPPOSE you have forgotten that
many weeks ago I promised to send
you an account of my companions at
the Wells. You would not deny me
a place among the most faithful votaries of idleness, if you knew how often I have recollected my
engagement, and contented myself to delay the
performance for some reason which I durst not
examine, because I knew it to be false ; how often
I have sat down to write, and rejoiced at interruption ; and how often I have praised the dignity of
resolution, determined at night to write in the

1 The only instances given in Johnson's *Dictionary* of
remains in the plural are in the sense of *the body left by the
soul.*

2 The news of Wolfe's conquest of Quebec and of his
death on the Heights of Abraham had reached England
scarcely more than a fortnight before this paper was published. Horace Walpole had written on October 21 :—" Our
bells are worn threadbare with ringing for victories."—
Walpole's *Letters*, iii. 259. Johnson was on one side, the
English nation on the other.

" Victrix causa deis placuit, sed victa Catoni."

morning, and referred it in the morning to the quiet hours of night.

I have at last begun what I have long wished at an end, and find it more easy than I expected to continue my narration.

Our assembly could boast no such constellation of intellects as Clarendon's band of associates. We had among us no Selden, Falkland, or Waller [1]; but we had men not less important in their own eyes, though less distinguished by the public ; and many a time have we lamented the partiality of mankind, and agreed that men of the deepest inquiry sometimes let their discoveries die away in silence, that the most comprehensive observers have seldom opportunities of imparting their remarks, and that modest merit passes in the crowd unknown and unheeded. [2]

One of the greatest men of the society was Sim Scruple, who lives in a continual equipoise of doubt, and is a constant enemy to confidence and dogmatism. Sim's favourite topic of conversation is the narrowness of the human mind, the fallaciousness of our senses, the prevalence of early prejudice, and the uncertainty of appearances. Sim has many doubts about the nature of death, and is sometimes inclined to believe that sensation

---

1 In Clarendon's *Autobiography*, published this year (see *ante*, *Idler*, No. 65), an account is given of " the men of more than ordinary eminence " in whose " conjunction and communication he took much delight."—*Life of the Earl of Clarendon*, ed. 1759, p. 19.

2   " Merit was ever modest known."
                     —Gay, *Court of Death*

may survive motion, and that a dead man may feel though he cannot stir. He has sometimes hinted that man might, perhaps, have been naturally a quadruped; and thinks it would be very proper, that at the Foundling Hospital some children should be inclosed in an apartment in which the nurses should be obliged to walk half upon four and half upon two, that the younglings, being bred without the prejudice of example, might have no other guide than nature, and might at last come forth into the world as genius should direct, erect or prone, on two legs or on four.

The next in dignity of mien and fluency of talk was Dick Wormwood, whose sole delight is to find every thing wrong. Dick never enters a room but he shews that the door and the chimney are ill-placed. He never walks into the fields but he finds ground ploughed which is fitter for pasture. He is always an enemy to the present fashion. He holds that all the beauty and virtue of women will soon be destroyed by the use of tea.[1] He triumphs when he talks on the present system

[1] Johnson is referring to Jonas Hanway, who had attacked the use of tea in his *Journal of Eight Days' Journey.* " Men," he wrote, " seem to have lost their stature and comeliness, and women their beauty. I am not young, but me thinks there is not quite so much beauty in this land as there was. Your very chambermaids have lost their bloom, I suppose by sipping tea." Johnson, in his review of this *Journal,* had owned himself "a hardened and shameless tea-drinker, who has for twenty years diluted his meals with only the infusion of this fascinating plant; whose kettle has scarcely time to cool; who with tea amuses the evening, with tea solaces the midnight, and with tea welcomes the morning."—Johnson's *Works,* vi. 21.

of education, and tells us with great vehemence, that we are learning words when we should learn things. He is of opinion that we suck in errors at the nurse's breast, and thinks it extremely ridiculous that children should be taught to use the right hand rather than the left.

Bob Sturdy considers it as a point of honour to say again what he has once said, and wonders how any man that has been known to alter his opinion can look his neighbours in the face. Bob is the most formidable disputant of the whole company ; for without troubling himself to search for reasons he tires his antagonist with repeated affirmations. When Bob has been attacked for an hour with all the powers of eloquence and reason, and his position appears to all but himself utterly untenable, he always closes the debate with his first declaration, introduced by a stout preface of contemptuous civility, "All this is very judicious ; you may " talk, Sir, as you please ; but I will still say what " I said at first." Bob deals much in universals which he has now obliged us to let pass without exceptions. He lives on an annuity, and holds that *there are as many thieves as traders ;* he is of loyalty unshaken, and always maintains, that *he who sees a Jacobite sees a rascal.*

Phil Gentle is an enemy to the rudeness of contradiction and the turbulence of debate. Phil has no notions of his own, and therefore willingly catches from the last speaker such as he shall drop. This inflexibility of ignorance is easily accommodated to any tenet ; his only difficulty is, when the disputants grow zealous, how to be of two contrary opinions at once. If no appeal is made to his judgment, he has the art of distributing his attention and his smiles in such a manner, that each thinks him of his own party; but if he is obliged to speak, he then observes that the question is difficult; that he never received so much pleasure from a debate before; that neither of the controvertists could have found his match in any other company; that Mr. Wormwood's assertion is very well supported, and yet there is great force in what Mr. Scruple advanced against it. By this indefinite declaration both are commonly satisfied; for he that has prevailed is in good humour; and he that has felt his own weakness is very glad to have escaped so well.

I am, Sir, yours, &c.

ROBIN SPRITELY.

No. 84. SATURDAY, NOVEMBER 24, 1759.

BIOGRAPHY is, of the various kinds of narrative writing, that which is most eagerly read, and most easily applied to the purpose of life.[1]

In romances, when the wild field of possibility lies open to invention, the incidents may easily be made more numerous, the vicissitudes more sudden, and the events more wonderful ; but from the time of life when fancy begins to be over-ruled by reason and corrected by experience, the most artful tale raises little curiosity when it is known to be false[2] ; but though it may, perhaps, be sometimes read as a model of a neat or elegant style, not for the sake of knowing what it contains, but how it is written ; or those that are weary of themselves, may have recourse to it as a pleasing dream, of which, when they awake, they voluntarily dismiss the images from their minds.

The examples and events of history press, indeed, upon the mind with the weight of truth,

1 See *ante*, *Rambler*, No. 60.

2 " It is somewhere recorded of a retired citizen that he was in the habit of again and again perusing *Robinson Crusoe* without a suspicion of its authenticity. At length a friend assured him of its being a work of fiction. ' What you say, replied the old man mournfully, ' may be true, but your information has taken away the only comfort of my age.' "—Johnson's *Works*, iv. 398, note by the Editor.

but when they are reposited in the memory, they are oftener employed for shew than use, and rather diversify conversation[1] than regulate life. Few are engaged in such scenes as give them opportunities of growing wiser by the downfall of statesmen or the defeat of generals. The stratagems of war, and the intrigues of courts, are read by far the greater part of mankind with the same indifference as the adventures of fabled heroes, or the revolutions of a fairy region. Between falsehood and useless truth there is little difference. As gold which he cannot spend will make no man rich, so knowledge which he cannot apply will make no man wise.

The mischievous consequences of vice and folly, of irregular desires and predominant passions, are best discovered by those relations which are levelled with the general surface of life, which tell not how any man became great, but how he was made happy; not how he lost the favour of his prince, but how he became discontented with himself.

Those relations are therefore commonly of most value in which the writer tells his own story.[2] He that recounts the life of another, commonly dwells most upon conspicuous events, lessens the familiarity of his tale to increase its dignity, shews his

1 Johnson in practice did not admit that it diversified conversation. " Sooner than hear of the Punic War he would be rude to the person that introduced the subject."—Boswell's *Johnson*, iii., 206, *note* 1.

2 Boswell refers to this passage in the beginning of his *Life of Johnson*.

favourite at a distance, decorated and magnified like the ancient actors in their tragic dress, and endeavours to hide the man that he may produce a hero.

But if it be true, which was said by a *French* prince, *That no man was a hero to the servants of his chamber,*[1] it is equally true, that every man is yet less a hero to himself. He that is most elevated above the crowd by the importance of his employments, or the reputation of his genius, feels himself affected by fame or business but as they influence his domestic life. The high and low, as they have the same faculties and the same senses, have no less similitude in their pains and pleasures.[2] The sensations are the same in all, though produced by very different occasions. The prince feels the same pain when an invader seizes a province, as the farmer when a thief drives away his cow. Men thus equal in themselves will appear equal in- honest and impartial biography ;

[1] " This phrase is commonly attributed to Mme. de Sévigné, but on the authority of Mme. Aisse belongs to Mme. Cornuel. ' Few men are admired by their servants.'—Montaigne, *Essays*, Bk. iii., chap. 11." Bartlett's *Familiar Quotations*, ed. 1888, p. 630. Carlyle remarks on this saying : —" It is not the Hero's blame, but the Valet's ; that his soul, namely, is a mean *valet*-soul. He expects his Hero to advance in royal stage-trappings, with measured step, trains borne behind him, trumpets sounding before him. It should stand rather, No man can be a *Grand-Monarque* to his valet-de-chambre."—*Lectures on Heroes*, ed. 1858, p. 322.

[2] " Shakespeare added drunkenness to the other qualities of the Danish usurper, knowing that kings love wine like other men, and that wine exerts its natural power upon kings."—Johnson's *Works*, v. 109.

and those whom fortune or nature place at the greatest distance may afford instruction to each other.

The writer of his own life has at least the first qualification of an historian, the knowledge of the truth ; and though it may be plausibly objected that his temptations to disguise it are equal to his opportunities of knowing it, yet I cannot but think that impartiality may be expected with equal confidence from him that relates the passages of his own life, as from him that delivers the transactions of another.

Certainty of knowledge not only excludes mistake, but fortifies veracity. What we collect by conjecture, and by conjecture only can one man judge of another's motives or sentiments, is easily modified by fancy or by desire ; as objects imperfectly discerned take forms from the hope or fear of the beholder. But that which is fully known cannot be falsified but with reluctance of understanding, and alarm of conscience : of understanding, the lover of truth ; of conscience, the sentinel of virtue.

He that writes the life of another is either his friend or his enemy, and wishes either to exalt his praise or aggravate his infamy ; many temptations to falsehood will occur in the disguise of passions, too specious to fear much resistance. Love of virtue will animate panegyric, and hatred of wickedness imbitter censure. The zeal of gratitude, the ardour of patriotism, fondness for an opinion, or fidelity to a party, may easily overpower the vigilance of a mind habitually well disposed, and prevail over unassisted and unfriended veracity.

But he that speaks of himself has no motive to falsehood or partiality except self-love, by which all have so often been betrayed, that all are on the watch against its artifices. He that writes an apology for a single action, to confute an accusation, to recommend himself to favour, is indeed always to be suspected of favouring his own cause ; but he that sits down calmly and voluntarily to review his life for the admonition of posterity, or to amuse himself, and leaves this account unpublished, may be commonly presumed to tell truth, since falsehood cannot appease his own mind, and fame will not be heard beneath the tomb.

No. 102. SATURDAY, MARCH 29, 1760.

I T very seldom happens to man that his business is his pleasure. What is done from necessity is so often to be done when against the present inclination, and so often fills the mind with anxiety, that an habitual dislike steals upon us, and we shrink involuntarily from the remembrance of our task. This is the reason why almost every one wishes to quit his employment ; he does not like another state, but is disgusted with his own.

From this unwillingness to perform more than is required of that which is commonly performed with reluctance, it proceeds that few authors write their own lives.[1] Statesmen, courtiers, ladies, generals, and seamen, have given to the world their own stories, and the events with which their different stations have made them acquainted. They retired to the closet as to a place of quiet and amusement, and pleased themselves with writing, because they could lay down the pen whenever they were weary. But the author, however conspicuous, or however important, either

---

[1] " It has been said there is pleasure in writing, particularly in writing verses. I allow you may have pleasure from writing after it is over, if you have written well ; but you don't go willingly to it again. I know when I have been writing verses, I have run my finger down the margin, to see how many I had made, and how few I had to make."—Boswell's *Johnson*, iv. 219.

in the public eye or in his own, leaves his life to be related by his successors, for he cannot gratify his vanity but by sacrificing his ease.

It is commonly supposed that the uniformity of a studious life affords no matter for narration : but the truth is, that of the most studious life a great part passes without study. An author partakes of the common condition of humanity; he is born and married like another man ; he has hopes and fears, expectations and disappointments, grief and joys, and friends and enemies, like a courtier or a statesman ; nor can I conceive why his affairs should not excite curiosity as much as the whisper of a drawing-room, or the factions of a camp.[1]

Nothing detains the reader's attention more powerfully than deep involutions of distress, or sudden vicissitudes of fortune ; and these might be abundantly afforded by memoirs of the sons of literature. They are entangled by contracts which they know not how to fulfil,[2] and obliged to

---

[1] " Somebody said, the life of a mere literary man could not be very entertaining. JOHNSON. ' But it certainly may. This is a remark which has been made, and repeated, without justice. Why should the life of a literary man be less entertaining than the life of any other man ? Are there not as interesting varieties in such a life ? As *a literary life* it may be very entertaining.'"—Boswell's *Johnson,* iv. 98. See *ante, The Rambler,* No. 60.

[2] " Old Gardner, the bookseller (said Johnson), employed Rolt and Smart to write a monthly miscellany, called *The Universal Visitor.* There was a formal written contract, which Allen, the printer, saw. . . . They were bound to write nothing else ; they were to have, I think, a third of the profits of this sixpenny pamphlet ; and the contract was for ninety-nine years."—Boswell's *Johnson,* ii. 345.

write on subjects which they do not understand. Every publication is a new period of time, from which some increase or declension of fame is to be reckoned. The gradations of a hero's life are from battle to battle, and of an author's from book to book.

Success and miscarriage have the same effects in all conditions. The prosperous are feared, hated, and flattered ; and the unfortunate avoided, pitied, and despised. No sooner is a book published than the writer may judge of the opinion of the world. If his acquaintance press round him in public places, or salute him from the other side of the street ; if invitations to dinner come thick upon him, and those with whom he dines keep him to supper ; if the ladies turn to him when his coat is plain, and the footmen serve him with attention and alacrity ; he may be sure that his work has been praised by some leader of literary fashions.

Of declining reputation the symptoms are not less easily observed. If the author enters a coffee-house, he has a box to himself ; if he calls at a bookseller's, the boy turns his back ; and, what is the most fatal of all prognostics, authors will visit him in a morning, and talk to him hour after hour of the malevolence of critics, the neglect of merit, the bad taste of the age, and the candour of posterity.

All this, modified and varied by accident and custom, would form very amusing scenes of bio-graphy, and might recreate many a mind which is very little delighted with conspiracies or battles, intrigues of a court, or debates of a parliament ;

to this might be added all the changes of the countenance of a patron, traced from the first glow
which flattery raises in his cheek, through ardour
of fondness, vehemence of promise, magnificence
of praise, excuse of delay, and lamentation of in-
ability, to the last chill look of final dismission,
when the one grows weary of soliciting and the
other of hearing solicitation.

Thus copious are the materials which have
been hitherto suffered to lie neglected, while the
repositories of every family that has produced a
soldier or a minister are ransacked, and libraries
are crowded with useless folios of state papers
which will never be read, and which contribute
nothing to valuable knowledge.

I hope the learned will be taught to know
their own strength and their value, and, instead
of devoting their lives to the honour of those
who seldom thank them for their labours,
resolve at last to do justice to themselves.

No. 103. SATURDAY, APRIL 5, 1760.

Respicere ad longæ jussit spatia ultima vitæ.—Juv.[1]

MUCH of the pain and pleasure of mankind arises from the conjectures which every one makes of the thoughts of others ; we all enjoy praise which we do not hear, and resent contempt which we do not see. The *Idler* may therefore be forgiven, if he suffers his imagination to represent to him what his readers will say or think when they are informed that they have now his last paper in their hands.

Value is more frequently raised by scarcity than by use. That which lay neglected when it was common, rises in estimation as its quantity becomes less. We seldom learn the true want of what we have till it is discovered that we can have no more.

This essay will, perhaps, be read with care even by those who have not yet attended to any other;

1 Juvenal, *Satires*, x. 275. Johnson in his *Vanity of Human Wishes* (l. 313) thus paraphrases the passage in which this line occurs:—

"*F*rom Lydia's monarch should the search descend,
  By Solon caution'd to regard his end,
  In life's last scenes what prodigies surprise,
  *F*ears of the brave, and follies of the wise !
  *F*rom Marlborough's eyes the streams of dotage flow,
  And Swift expires a driv'ller and a show."

and he that finds this late attention recompensed, will not forbear to wish that he had bestowed it sooner.

Though the *Idler* and his readers have contracted no close friendship, they are perhaps unwilling to part. There are few things not purely evil, of which we can say, without some emotion of uneasiness, *this is the last.*[1] Those who never could agree together, shed tears when mutual discontent has determined them to final separation ; of a place which has been frequently visited, though without pleasure, the last look is taken with heaviness of heart ; and the *Idler,* with all his chilliness of tranquillity, is not wholly unaffected by the thought that his last essay is now before him.

This secret horror of the last is inseparable from a thinking being, whose life is limited, and to whom death is dreadful.[2] We always make a secret comparison between a part and the whole ; the termination of any period of life reminds us that life itself has likewise its termination ; when we have done any thing for the last time, we involuntarily reflect that a part of the days allotted to us is past, and that as more is past there is less remaining.

It is very happily and kindly provided, that in

[1] Lord Eldon referred to this passage in a letter which he wrote to his daughter on taking his "farewell of office" as Lord Chancellor.—Twiss's *Life of Eldon*, ed. 1846, ii. 164.

"The horror of death which I had always observed in Dr. Johnson appeared strong to-night. . . . He said he never had a moment in which death was not terrible to him." —Boswell's *Johnson*, iii. 153.

every life there are certain pauses and interrup-
tions, which force consideration upon the careless,
and seriousness upon the light ; points of time
where one course of action ends, and another
begins ; and by vicissitudes of fortune, or alteration of employment, by change of place or loss of
friendship, we are forced to say of something, *this
is the last.*

An even and unvaried tenor of life[1] always hides
from our apprehension the approach of its end.
Succession is not perceived but by variation ; he
that lives to-day as he lived yesterday, and expects
that as the present day is such will be the morrow,
easily conceives time as running in a circle, and
returning to itself.   The uncertainty of our duration is impressed commonly by dissimilitude of
condition ; it is only by finding life changeable
that we are reminded of its shortness.

This conviction, however forcible at every new
impression, is every moment fading from the
mind ; and partly by the inevitable incursion of
new images, and partly by voluntary exclusion of
unwelcome thoughts,[2] we are again exposed to the
universal fallacy ; and we must do another thing
for the last time, before we consider that the time
is nigh when we shall do no more.

As the last *Idler* is published in that solemn
week which the Christian world has always set

1 " The noiseless tenor of their way " of *The Elegy in a
Country Churchyard*, is often misquoted " the even tenor."
Perhaps Gray's verse and Johnson's line become mingled in
the memory of their readers.

2 " The whole of life (said Johnson) is but keeping away
the thoughts of death."—Boswell's *Johnson*, ii. 93.

apart for the examination of the conscience, the review of life, the extinction of earthly desires, and the renovation of holy purposes ; I hope that my readers are already disposed to view every incident with seriousness, and improve it by meditation ; and that, when they see this series of trifles brought to a conclusion, they will consider that by outliving the *Idler*, they have passed weeks, months, and years, which are now no longer in their power ; that an end must in time be put to every thing great as to every thing little ; that to life must come its last hour, and to this system of being its last day, the hour at which probation ceases, and repentance will be vain ; the day in which every work of the hand, and imagination of the heart shall be brought to judgment, and an everlasting futurity shall be determined by the past.

WILLIAM RIDER & SON, PRINTERS, LONDON.

This book is DUE on the last
date stamped below

NOV 2 3 1934

OCT 2 6 1938

DEC 3 1 1949

JUL 2 1 1952

OCT 3 0 1952

NOV 2 1 1952

DEC 1 RECD

JAN 1 8 1956

MAY 1 6 1958

IN 1 8 10

Lightning Source UK Ltd.
Milton Keynes UK
UKHW01f0613210818
327557UK00010B/446/P